An Introduction to Political Theory

THE AUTHOR

CARL J. FRIEDRICH is Eaton Professor of the Science of Government at Harvard University. Since 1956, he has also held a professorship in political science at the University of Heidelberg, where he founded and continues to direct the *Institut fuer Politische Wissenschaft*. Professor Friedrich has written widely in political theory. His books include *Constitutional Government and Democracy, Inevitable Peace, The Philosophy of Kant, The Age of the Baroque, The Philosophy of Hegel, Totalitarian Dictatorship and Autocracy* (with Z. Brzezinski), *The Philosophy of Law in Historical Perspective, Transcendent Justice,* and *Man and His Government.*

Professor Friedrich is also a vice-president of the International Political Science Association and president-elect of the Institut International de Philosophie Politique. He is a past president of the American Political Science Association and of the American Society for Political and Legal Philosophy, and has served as a constitutional advisor to the American Military Governor in Germany (1946-1948), to Puerto Rico (1951 and later), and the European Constituent Assembly (1952-1953).

An Introduction to

Political Theory

TWELVE LECTURES AT HARVARD

Carl J. Friedrich

Harvard University

HARPER & ROW, PUBLISHERS

New York, Evanston, and London

An Introduction to Political Theory: Twelve Lectures at Harvard
Copyright © 1967 by C. J. Friedrich

LIBRARY OF CONGRESS CATALOG CARD NUMBER: 67–11648

C-R

Contents

Contents

Preface

The idea of preparing these twelve lectures, given once a week during the second half of the Harvard introductory course called Government 1, was first proposed by Mr. Rolin Posey, now at New College. They were first given in 1964, and reports about the students' keen interest caused Mr. Posey to suggest that they might be taped and prepared for publication. This was done in the spring of 1965 with the assistance of Professor Isaac Kramnick, now of Brandeis University. The Manuscript was edited by him and reviewed and revised by the author in the spring of 1966 while repeating their oral presentation. Obviously, they do not pretend to be anything but what the title indicates: an introduction for beginners into the vast and complex field of political theory. The very arrangement shows clearly that they are not intended as a survey of the history of political thought. Rather they select six basic and perennial problems of political argument and discussion, sketch, in one lecture, the nature of the issue and show, in another, how it was treated by one or two of the "classics" who have made a major contribution to this particular problem area. I am, of course, exceedingly grateful to Mr. Kramnick for all that he did to make me tighten the argument and to eliminate some of the more blatant extravagancies of popular speech which I am prone to commit. I am also much indebted to Mrs. Valerie Greenberg for her secretarial and editorial help. And last, but not least, to my helper of many years. It is my hope that these lectures may prove helpful to others engaged in similar tasks, as well as to their students; perhaps they too will come to feel the excitement which is aroused in me whenever I have to deal with one of the great issues of politics. Ours is a bitter time, and politics is proving the testing ground for all else. Its understanding is the "master science" once again, and its subject, as the Romans urged, "a hard matter." Indeed the future of all depends upon its grasp. The search for it is a never-ending quest.

C. J. FRIEDRICH

An Introduction to Political Theory

I

The Dimensions of Freedom

IN TACKLING THE PROBLEM of freedom and rights I would start by observing that this issue occupies the center of modern political thought. Ancient writers like Plato and Aristotle were not bothered by this problem. It is the modern theorist who asks how does one combine order with freedom? The Greeks, to be sure, called themselves the free, *hoi elentheroi*. Indeed they looked upon themselves as the only free men, contrasting themselves with the rest of mankind, *hoi barbaroi*. These latter were the aliens who could not share the intimate relationship with freedom which the Greeks claimed for themselves.

There is no more moving manifestation of this Greek idea of freedom than the celebrated funeral oration of Pericles as recorded in Thucydides. "In this land of ours which our ancestors transmitted to us as a free one," he proclaims. All through its moving sentences Pericles makes the idea of freedom the heart of his speech to the people gathered in the marketplace of Athens. These Athenians were the relatives and friends of men who had died in the Peloponnesian War, which in some ways was as unpopular in Athens as the Vietnam war is in America today. Then as now there was the same questioning, why, why, why should it be?

Pericles' great funeral oration was to some extent an attempt to answer this question in terms of the Athenians' love for and pride in freedom. Towards the end of his address Pericles says "Such is the city for which these men nobly fought and died," having linked the other values and convictions to that of freedom. Freedom is happiness and courage is freedom. And as free men, the Athenians can boldly assert: "We are lovers of beauty yet with no extravagance and lovers of wisdom yet without weakness." Freely spending they are too: "wealth we look upon rather as an opportunity for action than as a subject for boasting . . ." Hence Pericles considers Athens "the school of Hellas" and therefore "each man could in his own way prove himself self-sufficient. . . ."

This reference to self-sufficiency did not mean, however, that Pericles and the Athenians had the modern idea of personal liberty. Freedom for the Greek clearly had primarily the one dimension of his polis being fully independent and not subject to any outside power. This is not far from what developing nations today mean when they speak of freedom—freedom as self-sufficiency, independence, standing on one's own feet. The other dimension of freedom for Pericles meant the ability to participate in political life. The free man was the active citizen who helped shape the laws and policies of the Polis.

In the west the ideal of freedom is personal and related to the individual himself. In a sense this has its origins in the freedom of religion, the right to believe. Its roots are in the Christian faith and traditions. In the early writings of St. Augustine one finds the recognition that people in order to be real men must be free in their convictions, must be free to believe what they really believe. The Christian doctrine is that faith cannot be forced, that conversion must rest on persuasion and can never be based on coercion.

There are other roots of such a personal conception of freedom. It is an error to think that freedom of religion is the sole basis of human rights. Equally important is the protection of property. The constitutional documents of seventeenth-century England are full of provisions regarding property. This is the feudal heritage; freedom to own a certain amount of property is seen as a necessary condition for being able to maintain personal independence.

Closely related to this distinctly western notion of personal freedom is the idea of human rights proclaimed in a very special sense for the first time in the Magna Carta of 1215. This was no universal declaration of human rights such as that proclaimed by the United Nations in 1949. The Great Charter of the thirteenth century refers to the particular rights of particular persons, the barons and high clergy in Britain who objected to the King's claim of absolute power over them. It was a limited charter of very special freedoms. Yet it included some rights of freemen, of free Englishmen. Therefore it is still entitled to the honors it has received; it contained the seed that ultimately grew into the universal declaration of human rights of the twentieth century. One great link was forged in the seventeenth century when lawyers like Sir Edward Coke made the Magna Carta the foundation for the Bill of Rights of 1628 as well as a number of other bills formulated during the Revolution.

In these bills you find the characteristic western combination of something very material, the rights of property, with something very spiritual, the right of religion. In between these rights, and equally important, appear the procedural personal rights like the right of habeas corpus and the right to a trial by jury, a trial by men equal to oneself, by one's peers, as the old phrase has it. A word about jury trial. Trial by jury means less chance of blunder, since it is a trial by men familiar with your background and beliefs. The idea is to prevent injustice done out of ignorance of the motivation of men being tried. The entire notion of human rights, religious, proprietary and procedural, is associated with the idea that freedom is of the essence of man, seen as an individual person. It has come to be associated with the idea of a constitution which spells out these rights. The first attempt at such spelling out occurred in England in the Revolutionary era with Cromwell's *Instrument of Government* (1653) attempting an elaborate written constitution. There followed, of course, the more drastic efforts in 1787 and 1789, and others down to this very day.

One of the main points I want to make is that this idea of hu-

man rights has undergone a very striking evolution since the eighteenth century. Until that time the prevailing notion was that of
natural rights, rights based on human nature and thus unalterable
and inalienable. This is the notion which underlies the first ten
amendments to the American Constitution which contains a good
many of what we recognize as basic American rights. Since that
time the idea of guaranteeing personal freedom has undergone a
dramatic development which in a sense is a shift in emphasis
which is expressed in our vocabulary. In the nineteenth century
people came to talk more and more of liberties rather than of
rights. More important, in particular they talked about civil liberties. With the forward march of democracy in America in the
second half of the nineteenth century the liberties connected with
political participation came to the fore. Such civil liberties were
being looked upon as all-important. It was no longer possible to
talk in respectable intellectual circles of natural rights. Then in the
twentieth century, there occurred a third shift. President Franklin
Roosevelt issued a famous declaration of "four freedoms," not
liberties but freedoms. Between 1787 and 1947 a transformation
had taken place from natural rights to civil liberties to human
freedoms.

What does this evolution indicate, what does it mean? As you
know, when speech is changed thoughts have changed, have become different. The stress on civil liberties as contrasted with that
on natural rights is actually indicative of a move to a different
dimension of freedom, one which had been of primary importance
to the ancient Greeks. Natural rights refer to rights *against* the
government, to the freedom of independence. Human beings
insist on having it recognized that a personal sphere exists which
government cannot invade. This is the dimension of freedom as
independence. Civil liberties, on the other hand, point toward that
dimension of freedom which is concerned with how human beings
can participate in civil government. It is not concerned with independence from government but with participation *in* government. This dimension of freedom is concerned not with persons
by themselves apart but with citizens in the midst of political
activity.

Now look at President Roosevelt's proclamation of the four freedoms. It speaks primarily of human freedoms not rights. You find that the older notions of rights and liberties have been contracted into two of his four freedoms. Freedom of expression which is a more general word for the right of religion also includes other kinds of convictions and the means of expressing them and thus refers to free speech and generally freedom of expression. There is also freedom of participation in the community to which most of the civil liberties are contracted. But much more important really than these two links with older traditions is that Roosevelt referred to two new freedoms—freedom from want and freedom from fear. These two refer neither to human beings by themselves nor to human beings participating in politics and government, but rather to human beings who must be protected against something, against fear, against want. We have here a totally different dimension of freedom when the talk is of freedom *through* government, that is freedoms which men can only attain with the help of their government.

Freedom from want is of course today epitomized in the quest for the Great Society but its achievement has preoccupied men throughout this century. It has taken the form of guaranteeing, for example, the right to work, or full employment, which provides human beings not merely with right to own property but more essentially with economic security. Now what of freedom from fear, what does this mean? It means freedom from the fear of being killed in war; it is the freedom which calls for something more than existing government can provide, such as world-wide organization in order to eliminate the danger of war. Thus you can see how alteration in the terminology symbolizes an alteration in point of view.

The entire development from rights through civil liberties to human freedoms is epitomized in the Declaration of Human Rights of 1949. The declaration recognizes the two dimensions of freedom in terms of independence and participation but it also proclaims a third dimension. What should this dimension be called? It encompasses the development of creativity or the effective capacity of men to unfold their personalities. It is the freedom of men to be fully themselves and not to be cramped by the fear of war or by poverty and disease which prevents human beings from realizing their full potential. This dimension of freedom calls for social security, for work, for education, and rest. It requires a rich cultural life and internal order. All of these are now a part of freedom. We can also say, putting these three dimensions another way, that rights related to oneself instead of to the government are self-conserving; such are the rights of freedom of independence. Or they might be self-asserting as are the rights of freedom of participation. Or, finally, they are self-developing rights which comprise the freedom of creation and innovation. Political freedom is never again going to appear satisfactory unless it is concerned with each one of these dimensions. We are never again going to have people satisfied merely with freedom of independence, nor satisfied merely with freedom of participation, as were our forebears. People will ask for some of both and they will go even beyond that.

There are a number of points which I think we should take up in connection with this evolution of the beliefs about freedom and the rights and liberties which express it. First of all, you can clearly see that this development goes far beyond the age of modern liberalism. It has roots deep in the past and yet it points far beyond liberalism into the future. The universal declaration of the United Nations, for example, was worked out in a long series of discussions between the Soviet Union, the United States and all other countries in the United Nations. It is therefore not merely a result of liberal views. It was only after protracted negotiations that formulations satisfactory to all participants could be found. One of the difficulties in the discussion between ourselves and the men of the East is that when we say we are the free and you are not, they say no, quite on the contrary, we are the free, you are the slaves. You are the slaves of capitalism, whereas we have true freedom. At international meetings at which the Soviet Union is represented one discovers that they put much greater stress on the freedom of creation, freedom from want and freedom from fear, whereas we stress the freedom of independence. With respect to freedom of participation, I think at present the scales are about balanced. They are proud that the people they really care about, the class-conscious elements of the proletariat, organized in the Communist Party, enjoy really extensive participation. We are prouder that everyone participates, although we are not so sure that the participation is always very impressive. We worry about the low percentages of participation in elections. When we talk about what we should do about it, some say we should make voting compulsory, while others say this is an invasion of freedom and arguments become somewhat involved.

The next point is quite tricky. The question may be raised as to whether there are rights only when the people who personally have the rights are aware that they exist or whether these rights have objective existence independent of subjective recognition. You may consider this an abstract and theoretical question but it really is at the very heart of the great struggle being waged in this country by the Negro to improve his position in American society. What the Supreme Court said in its decisions in the 50's is that people had been mistaken about the Constitution. The rights which we now recognize the Negro to have are rights which have always been in the Constitution although they have hitherto not been fully appreciated. The fact that it could be argued that Negroes themselves were not aware that these rights existed is no valid argument. They existed because they are recognized in the Constitution. But it is not only because of their recognition in the Constitution that these rights exist; after all the Constitution is merely a creation of men, of human beings bringing subjective insights to bear. No, the underlying belief is that these rights were always there and that the Constitution merely made them explicit. So that you can see that there still persists this older notion of human rights as natural human rights. Indeed, there are quite a few modern instances of this explicit recognition of natural rights. For example, the constitution in post-war Italy and Germany explicitly states that the rights therein contained are inalienable and inviolable. Any violation of them is merely a failure to execute, to enforce; the right itself cannot be affected; it continues to exist.

One important objection to such a view is that the very historical development which I have sketched for you suggests an evolution in what men take to be the rights or the freedoms of human beings. Furthermore, what should we make of the fact that some rights are recognized in some jurisdictions and some in other jurisdictions? Let me give you an illustration. The Germans are very keen about academic freedom and they have very explicitly recognized in their Constitution for many years that there is a right of teachers and students in universities to be entirely free. Academic freedom is a very important and central human right to the German. They describe it as "freedom to teach and freedom to learn." This right, however, has not been made much of in this country. The federal constitution does not speak of it and only a few states' constitutions allude to it; even the new Puerto Rican Constitution does not, and when it was suggested, they emphatically rejected the notion. This is curious, since in fact academic freedom has become an important issue with us. Almost the only mention of academic freedom in an American constitutional document is found in this Commonwealth, Massachusetts, but only for Harvard College! This Constitution was drawn up by people who had seen a good deal of religious conflict and they were very much concerned with the right to express conviction.

No two constitutions are in fact identical as to their bills of rights. There are innumerable and often quite curious differences between them. The Bavarians, jolly and nature-loving as they are, saw fit to guarantee every man the right to enjoy the beauties of nature. On a more serious level, a bill of rights really calls for spelling out in some detail what it is that a given political community particularly cherishes. The Puerto Ricans, progressively led and world-conscious in their outlook, wanted to embody in their constitution many of the new freedoms which had found a place in the universal declaration. The American Congress disallowed a number of these as not compatible with the American tradition. I believe they were quite mistaken about that; these freedoms had found a place in a number of American state constitutions, but not in a majority of them and that was decisive, along with the argument that Puerto Rico did not have the wherewithal to implement these rights. It is an objection which troubles many of the developing countries. For obviously the new freedoms, the freedoms which embody rights that can only be attained through governmental action, presuppose a strong government with ample resources. But the primary issue is that of the community's beliefs. That is why debates concerning a bill of rights are apt to become so protracted, and frequently so very bitter. For the consensus in a political community is never complete, as it is never permanent. As communities differ from one another in values and beliefs their constitutions reflect this. It stands to reason that as communities develop they form new values and preferences and their bills of rights will to some extent reflect this evolution.

Because of this difference in time and in place it might be difficult to insist that rights exist apart from their recognition by those who benefit from them. Yet I would be inclined to say that they do, though not absolutely, but politically. It is necessary that the existence of these rights be recognized by the political community in which they are to exist. It is *not* necessary for these rights to be recognized by the person to whom they apply. In other words, what the Supreme Court is saying is that the American people, when they put down certain particular rights in the Bill of Rights, made them come into being, made them the prevailing norms in the United States, even though Negroes did not realize they applied to them. Principles that rights, liberties and freedom embody are dependent upon the community that recognizes the rights, not on the individuals to whom they apply.

Another question, equally important and equally difficult, which emerges from this discussion is whether there is or should be a rank order among rights. Does one right have a priority over another right when, as always happens, rights come into conflict with one another? In this country at the present time there are some who say that the recent civil rights legislation which gives the Negro the right to stay in inns deprives the proprietor of some of his property rights. This is perfectly true. Recognizing the right of everyone to stay in certain places does restrict property rights. Indeed this is one of the most ancient of restrictions on property rights for it is an injunction of the common law that the keeper of an inn must take in everyone who comes to his door. He only had the right to keep an inn if he would make it available to any traveler on the King's highway. This is a good example of conflict in rights. Others can easily be found. The right of free speech often conflicts with other rights. Which right has priority over the other? My own belief is that there is no definite clear-cut answer. There is no definite rank order. People have at various times tried in the United States to describe such an order. It has been suggested, for example, that the rights of the first amendment have priority over the rights in other amendments, or that they follow each other in order of importance. But this does not work, nor is there evidence that they were arranged with a view to priority. Furthermore, what of the several rights in the first amendment? How are they to be ranked? Such emphasis placed on the first amendment also does not help us with regard to the crucially important rights embodied in the Constitution. Are they to be ranked higher or less high? How does the right of habeas corpus compare to due process?

The people who wrote the Bill of Rights never thought in terms of rank. The Anglo-American tradition is not to argue over an inherent rank order. Rather than trying to figure out a priority of rights it has sought to organize procedures for settling specific cases, for deciding which right has preference over another at any one time in any one concrete case. In a particular case, an inherently important right may be involved in a small way whereas a lesser right is involved in a big way, so that it outweighs the more important one. Hence we have a system of courts set up to weigh the conflict of rights and to decide in each case how rights should be ranked in the particular situation.

This last point brings to mind once more the problem of enforcement which is important in connection with all questions of freedom and rights. Mention of the courts illustrates the dependence of all rights upon the potentialities of enforcement. Rights without remedy are not very useful rights to anyone. The reason why most of us do not put much stake in the universal declaration of the United Nations is precisely because in contrast to our Bill of Rights it has no enforcement machinery. It is one thing for the United States and the U.S.S.R. to agree on the right to work but another for them to agree on how such rights should be enforced. We thus encounter the problem of political order. Rights exist only within the context of a political order wherein they can be enforced. Freedom thus presupposes order. It might appear that order and freedom are contradictory, but in reality there cannot be freedom without a certain order and what is more there cannot be order without a measure of freedom. The fact that all rights in order to be provided with remedies presuppose enforcement machinery explains why the west, in developing its great traditions of freedom and rights, had to develop and did indeed develop its great tradition of constitutional government.

There is another point which I want to mention, and that is the necessity to be alert to emerging rights. If it is true, as I have suggested, and as I think the evidence supports, that rights are expressive of values and beliefs prevalent in a community, then as the values and beliefs in a community change there must also occur a change in the rights found in that community. The formulation of the provisions for human rights must be made flexible. One must not start from the premise so very prevalent and indeed still expressed in the Constitution that rights are inalienable and unalterable. We must be aware that this is not so. The right of private property as it was understood in the past is still recognized but in Socialist Yugoslavia it means something very different from what it meant in the eighteenth century. The property right has universally, not only in Yugoslavia, been gradually reduced, and more and more the idea has come forward that this right is only acceptable when it is associated with obligations. Any possession of property thus recognizes the obligation that this property should be put to satisfactory uses. This is a radical change from the concept of property rights of the seventeenth century. Another example of such emerging reformation is the right of free association which is the basis of the trade union movement in all modern industrial nations. It is not recognized in the American federal Constitution, but recognition is found in a few state constitutions and it is becoming acceptable in the United States though even now the battle goes on over Section 14B of the Taft-Hartley Act and efforts are being made in quite a few states to pass legislation that affects union organization.

Evolution of values and beliefs means conflict and disagreement in the community. We can start, I think, with the assumption that a political community is in agreement on some values and beliefs but we must also assume that while most support the consensus there may be some dissent. When this is creative dissent pointing ahead and anticipating future developments it may well crystallize into new and different rights. One such prospect is academic freedom which as I suggested is something becoming increasingly important in the United States. It has not yet progressed to that point where it is seen as a central and important right. It is usually not seen as a separate right but as included in the right of free speech. I would suggest that if it is denied explicit recognition it is more appropriate to put academic freedom under the right of religion because it relates to conviction. When I am called professor I am spoken of as a man who professes, from the Latin word which means to confess. In the term professor derived from medieval universities there is inherent recognition that the men who stand on the academic platform are people who should be true to convictions, the first of which, of course, is the dedication to truth.

This steady development of rights as values and beliefs change is an ongoing process. Thus in the Universal Declaration of Human Rights we find one package of rights described and in the Yugoslavian Constitution we find a different package and in the Federal Republic of Germany yet another one. Each of these bills is an expression of a particular stage of evolution in the particular community quite apart from what is enforced and what is not.

The final point of this analysis of the dimensions of freedom is that one need recognize that freedom is not primarily a qualitative term. Men are not either "free" or "not free." Man may be free in one way and yet not in another. One can be *more* or *less* free. Americans before 1941 were freer than during the war. They were freer after 1945 than they had been before. Germans today are freer than they were thirty years ago. In other words we have ongoing changes in the degree of freedom. This is very important. Freedom is not an absolute and purely qualitative something; it is a relative thing. In this connection there is one concluding thought I want to leave with you, which may find you in violent disagreement. The great tradition of liberalism holds that not only should freedom be maximized, but also that all people want it maximized. Experience in the last one hundred years has shown this to be quite in error. In the first place, people do not want freedom to be maximized. Actually I think it is much more nearly true to say that people want a minimum of freedom, rather than a maximum. Most people are very glad to leave a lot of things to other people. If you say you are being interfered with, they say that they are glad to be interfered with, that they do not want to be concerned with all the decisions that they would have to make if they took advantage of all the different freedoms. It is even doubtful that one ought to say that freedom ought to be maximized. In this connection there is the question of man's capacity for freedom. After all, each time a man gets a new freedom he also has to make a lot of new decisions. Is he capable of making them? Should he really have to face so many decisions which he then needs to think about?

Such questions are a clear indication that a good political order which provides a certain amount of freedom for everybody is by no means a political order in which the maximum amount of freedom is provided for everybody. If human beings achieve freedom in one area they may lessen their freedom in another. They may also lose very easily and quickly the amount of freedom they have won in long struggles. I have opened up these many issues not because I feel I can settle them but to start the debate and invite you to argue and discuss freedom in its several dimensions and to reach your own conclusions.

2

The Doctrine of Liberalism:

Locke and Mill

FREEDOM, like all the great basic values of humankind, is no modern invention nor restricted to any particular time and place. Friedrich Schiller was right when he sang: "Be embracéd, all ye millions, one great kiss to all the world." And yet, we owe it to modern liberalism to have made this value the center of political teachings. Never before had all other concerns of man been highlighted in terms of this one all-absorbing question: how can men be given the chance to achieve freedom, not for some chosen ones, but for all? How must a political society be organized to make this possible? Nor had political thinkers before the great liberal movement penetrated to the heart of how freedom is related to order, and therefore to law. That the value of order has limits, has always been apparent to those who value freedom. That freedom in turn depends upon a measure, a degree of order, has been stressed by all who have argued about freedom under law. But this freedom which has been at the heart of such a large portion of political thought and action in the last three hundred years, is the hard core of the doctrine of political liberalism.

I am undertaking the first of the historical companion lectures, having talked to you before on the problem of freedom and rights in the general terms it presents itself to us today. I want now to go into what one might call the doctrinal aspect of the problem, more particularly the thought of two writers, Locke and Mill, who figure prominently in your reading.

I think it might be interesting to start this discussion of the doctrine of liberalism with an observation of a more general kind. Liberalism is, or at least was until very recently in the United States, a praise word of such general appeal that the tendency in the United States was, and still is to a certain extent in public writings, to obscure its historical meaning by applying it to practically all political doctrines. Twenty years ago it was particularly striking that liberalism seemed to be at the same time the doctrine of Herbert Hoover's rugged individualism and the doctrine of the *Daily Worker* expounding the Marxist faith. All of these claimed to be liberals. What this signifies is that in the United States everybody wanted to associate himself and his program with this highly desirable general name. In this respect American experience is quite different from European. In France and Germany liberalism is sort of dated and much less enthusiastically evoked. As a historical category it is related to the bourgeoisie and Babbitry. It even carries with it the connotation of nineteenth century humanitarian sentimentality. This very different attitude toward liberalism in Europe, which was already true forty or fifty years ago, is essentially a result of the challenge of Marxism which I expect to elaborate later. This different appreciation of liberalism may also have something to do with the fact that some of the greatest writers on the doctrine of liberalism were English and American and never achieved the kind of universal popularity on the continent which they did achieve in this country and in England.

I might mention, at least in passing, that there has recently been a revival of liberalism on the continent of Europe, doctrinally designated as neo-liberalism. This new school transcends, to some extent, the predominant doctrine of liberalism in the nineteenth century with its emphasis on laissez-faire, "let alone" individualism. Neo-liberalism accepts the need for a strong state to cope with monopoly power and other abuses of liberty by economic and social forces. This neo-liberalism is, in a sense, a response to a response. Laissez-faire liberalism elicited the challenge of socialism and Marxism which we will discuss later. In response to this response neo-liberalism arose after the second World War as an alternative to the totalitarianism spawned by socialism and Marxism.

John Locke is undoubtedly the most important of the great writers on liberalism. His dates are 1632 to 1704. He is thus clearly a man of the seventeenth century. Locke has been called the soul of liberalism because it is said that he makes freedom the supreme end of government. In making freedom the supreme end of government Locke, in a sense, secularized Protestantism. Luther had called himself Luther the free, because he considered the freedom of the Christian man the very heart of his doctrine in which he challenged ecclesiastical authority. I think this matter of challenging authority, ecclesiastical and lay, lies close to the heart of the doctrine of liberalism as expounded in the past. This anti-authority emphasis is, however, not the sole ingredient of liberal thought. Liberalism at the same time has many other facets. It has been affected both in time and in place by distinctive features of national culture. Indeed, one significant writer on liberalism, the Italian, de Ruggiero, has actually made the differentiation of national cultures the basis of his analysis of liberalism. He treats the doctrine in terms of English liberalism, French liberalism, German liberalism and Italian liberalism. He has endeavored to show that liberalism in each of these national cultures had a distinctive flavor reflecting its geographical and cultural home. In our discussion we will focus on English and American liberalism, the liberalism of the English speaking world.

Locke, curiously enough, stands between the two historical schools of liberalism. He is neither an old liberal nor a neoliberal, but something still more archaic. Neo-liberalism fights the kind of liberalism that we find in the elder Mill or in Jefferson and Paine. Their doctrine is well expressed in the idea of the state as night watchman. Tom Paine has put the old liberal doctrine especially well in his *Common Sense,* a tremendously popular book at the time of the writing of the American Constitution. I will cite for you one key sentence from it. "Society in every state is a blessing; but government even in its best state is but a necessary evil." This kind of sentiment has its roots in ancient doctrines of Christianity although it is here stated in a strictly secular form. It leads to the conclusion that that government is best which governs least. In his *Rights of Man* Paine reinforced the argument. I cite from this latter work one other statement: "The more perfect civilization is, the less occasion has it for government because the more does it regulate its own affairs and govern itself." In Paine's view a few general laws is all that civilized life requires. Civilized life is thus characterized by the gradual disappearance of the need for government and of the need for laws. We in the twentieth century are apt to throw up our hands and exclaim "What naïveté!" We have witnessed in connection with the forward movement of civilization an ever greater multiplication of laws and an ever greater extension of governmental activity. At the beginning of the modern age the liberal sentiment was just the opposite—the more civilization advances, the less need there will be for government and law. John Locke, in a sense the very "soul" of liberalism, did not have such an illusion. Locke saw government as very important and very necessary for realizing liberty. Laws were the perfect focus and the primary expression of such government. So let us turn to this doctrine of Locke which you are reading in his *Second Treatise on Civil Government.* I would like to highlight for you here those parts of the *Treatise* which relate to the particular problem of freedom.

I think we should first take up the problem of freedom and property. In recent years this has been a very important source of controversy in connection with the argument of socialism. Locke, however, uses the term property in two rather different senses.

He uses it in a very wide sense and he also uses it in a narrower and more restricted sense. When Locke uses the term "property" in its widest sense it is coincident with freedom. Liberty is a part of property. Property in the very wide sense of all that belongs to a man obviously includes life, a man's personal body, liberty, in the sense of all the different things he might want to do, and estate. As Locke puts it in a number of places, property is all-inclusive. Life, liberty, and estate are involved in the broad meaning of property. But there is also the narrower and more ordinary understanding of property. In this sense property is understood as a means to achieve freedom. Locke goes one step farther and even implies in his discussion that only men of property care for freedom. Thus one finds an élitist and exclusive dimension in Locke's discussion of freedom. But this is another of these contradictions in which the *Civil Government* of Locke is so rich, for there is also an egalitarian side to Locke's thinking which comes out when we face the next problem in connection with freedom, the state of nature.

Locke describes the state of nature as the state of perfect freedom. What does the "state of nature" mean and what does it mean to say that it is the state of perfect freedom? Locke describes the state of nature as the condition of perfect freedom because in it he sees each man free to order his actions and dispose of his possessions and person as he thinks fit. For this reason man in such a situation is perfectly free. There is, however, a limit to this perfect freedom, which is very important to Locke's doctrine of freedom. Natural man is free only within the bounds of the law of nature. This law of nature is the third aspect of Locke's doctrine of freedom.

Locke writes that the law of nature obliges everyone. Very well, it obliges everyone—but what is it? What is its content? Locke's answer is a very broad one. The law of freedom is reason. What does this reason do? Locke tells us that it teaches all mankind that since all men are equal and independent, no one man ought to harm another in his life, health, liberty or possessions. When asked why this should be so, Locke offers a quasi-religious answer.

All men are God's creatures he affirms. God is their maker; therefore men are God's possessions. By this very law of reason which forbids one to invade someone else's possessions, we must not harm other people. To do so would be to invade God's possession and we would be taking something from God that is his.

This idea that there is a law of nature which is a law of reason has a long history. It is by no means a novel idea of Locke's. The roots of natural law thinking extend on the one hand to classical antiquity and the ideas of the Stoics, Cicero, and the Roman Law. Its other, and in some ways an even more important root, is in the doctrine of Christianity. There is one particular passage which is a famous *locus classicus* for this Christian origin of the doctrine of the law of nature. You find it in *Romans, Chapter II, verse 14* where St. Paul is concerned with the importance of law. He says there, "When gentiles who have not the law" (by gentiles he means non-Jews) "when gentiles who have not the law, do by nature what the law requires, they are a law unto themselves, even though they do not have the law." There is an idea that is implanted in men's minds, in their reason, which resembles the law of Christ. This is the law of nature. When the gentiles act in accordance with this law of nature, they are a law unto themselves. It is important to realize that Locke is thus very squarely in the Christian tradition when he sets forth these ideas of natural law in abstract, general, and philosophic terms. Locke adds, however, a new element to the natural law doctrine which you do not find in St. Paul or in the early Christian tradition. This addition is connected with the state of nature, in which this law of nature operates. It is found in Locke's effort to answer the questions, "Who executes this law of nature? Who enforces it?" In the answer which Locke gives is his novel contribution to natural law thinking. Execution of the law of nature is put into every man's hands. Everyone has a right to punish the transgressors of that law. The basis for this assertion that the law of nature's enforcement is put into every man's hands is the assumption that the law would be in vain if there were no one to enforce it. For Locke, then, the law of nature is not something that automatically realizes itself, as seems to be implied in that citation from St. Paul, and which was also implied in the doctrine of the Stoics.

A serious objection arises at this point. If everyone is to enforce the law of nature with reference to injuries to himself, and to others, but more particularly when the individual is himself to judge whether he was hurt by another man, does this not make men judges in their own cases? To an Englishman this is, of course, a very serious thing. Over many years and many generations, Englishmen had developed the idea that it was a very bad legal system in which men were judges in their own cases. In such a situation there is the distinct danger that men will abuse their power. Far from restricting themselves as they ought to by the enforcement of the law of nature, they will use these occasions to transgress the law of nature and to appropriate to themselves what is another's. From this it would seem that Locke comes pretty close to the idea of the law of the war of all against all which had been so important for Hobbes. But Locke really doesn't make this assumption. He is rescued from this Hobbesian image because he thinks most men are fairly pleasant chaps. Most men don't go in for this fighting. There are, to be sure, some wicked men, however, men who will take advantage of just such a situation. It is the activity of this evil minority which makes the state of nature intolerable. In the state of nature there is no common judge to discipline such men and to decide disputes which they create. It is to set up this judge that men enter civil government, the next step in Locke's argument.

Before I turn to that, however, I want to point out one other thing. Locke faced the important question critics raised against this idea of a state of nature, its historical reality. Was there ever any such state? His answer, as was Hobbes', was the suggestion that his critic look at rulers of independent nations. These rulers of independent nations, Locke suggested, were surely in a state of nature. In addition to this, Locke hints that the state of nature is a useful construct which gives us an opportunity to identify and isolate the basis of government and obligation. It is also helpful in enabling us to identify the primary objective of government which is freedom. Freedom can only be made secure by civil government. One additional point Locke makes on this problem of the historical reality of the state of nature is an allusion to newly colonized America and its Indian tribes.

You can see here that there is an unresolved difficulty in Locke's thinking. Whereas he started out by saying that the state of nature is the state of perfect freedom, it appears now that it isn't so perfect. It appears that it is even necessary to set up a civil government and get away from this state of nature in order to achieve freedom. I think there is no real answer to this contradiction except to say that good old John Locke has slipped. What he really wanted to say was that the state of nature could be the state of perfect freedom if only men would be what they ought to be. But they are not.

It follows from what we now know of Locke's views that there can be no use in his theory for the establishment of an absolute monarchy. He makes it quite clear that absolute monarchy along the lines of what Hobbes had proposed would leave men in the state of nature vis-à-vis the one to whom they had given absolute power. This monarch would surely be a judge in his own case. All the others would be delivered up into his hands without defense. A civil government must, therefore, provide for a separation or division of power. Locke never wearies of insisting that concentrated power is the death of freedom. In this doctrine he articulates a distrust of all power holders which has its root in Christian doctrine. Much later in the nineteenth century Lord Acton, a liberal Catholic of great intellectual stature, wrote in a letter to a friend the famous statement, "All power tends to corrupt and absolute power corrupts absolutely." This typically liberal statement is a radicalization of the basic Christian idea that in all fallen men is some evil and that the abuse of power is thus something with which one must reckon whenever one gives power to any human being.

In this connection I would like to call your attention to a passage which occurs in the writings of a later follower of Locke, the

Utilitarian James Mill, the father of John Stuart Mill. James Mill wrote an *Essay on Government* which is quite interesting and attractive if only because it is brief. Trying to buttress the idea that human beings are prone to be corrupted by power and to abuse it, Mill introduces a notion which I think is very touchingly British. "The world affords some decisive experiments upon human nature in exact conformity with this conclusion that power is abused. An English gentleman may be taken as a favorable specimen of civilization, of knowledge, of humanity, of all the qualities in short that make human nature estimable. The degree in which he desires to possess power over his fellow creatures, and the degree of oppression to which he finds motives for carrying the exercise of that power will afford a standard from which assuredly there can be no appeal." In short what Mill is suggesting is that if even Britishers fall prey to this propensity of men to seek and abuse power, then surely this is a universal law of human nature. What does he use as illustration? He chooses the conduct of British gentlemen in India and other colonies. Here the passage is quite illuminating. "But yet it is true that these propensities led English gentlemen not only to deprive their slaves of property and to make property of their fellow creatures, but to treat them with a degree of cruelty, the very description of which froze the blood of those of their countrymen who were placed in less unfavourable circumstances, namely, staying at home and not being exposed to these temptations of power."

You have here, I think, the supporting evidence for the distrust of power which, and I cite once again James Mill, "creates the great difficulty." All the difficult questions of government relate to the means of restraining from making bad use of it those in whose hands is lodged the power necessary for the protection of all. The answer of John Locke was the separation of powers, a constitutional government in which power is carefully divided. All I want to say to you on this intrinsically complicated subject for which one would need an entire hour is that John Locke doesn't use the pattern which is familiar to us from Montesquieu and our own constitution, namely a separation between the executive, the legislative and the judicial. The judicial does not even turn up in Locke; but rather he is insistent upon dividing the legislative power among several authorities. More particularly he suggests quite within the tradition of English government, to divide it between the King, the Lords and the Commons. Only if power in general and legislative power, in particular, which is the crucial power, is thus divided, can men hope to be free.

If we turn to the later liberals and more particularly to John Stuart Mill, we find that the position has radically changed. The problem of freedom is no longer the problem of how to protect men against the abuse of power by government, but how to protect men against the abuse of power by others than those in the government. A result of this change is the necessity of activating government for the purpose of producing this restraint. Let me first point out to you that before the statement of this basic problem in John Stuart Mill's *On Liberty,* another significant shift had occurred in the liberal doctrine. The Utilitarians, of whom Bentham was the founder and John Stuart Mill perhaps the most impressive, certainly the most universally significant expounder, had abandoned the idea of the separation of powers. Bentham thunders against the separation of powers as endangering government by the division of authority. Yet Bentham remained aware of the problem of effective restraints upon power. He remained aware of the problem of dividing power. The solution for Bentham and the utilitarians, and this is the key point of James Mill's *Essay on Government* from which I quoted to you, is, however, representative government. As James Mill says in this essay representative government is "the grand discovery of modern times." An elective government, in which representatives are chosen for a limited period of time is the desirable check upon the abuse of power by the executive establishment.

These ideas of James Mill were elaborated by his famous son, John Stuart Mill, in an essay called *Considerations on Representative Government.* It is an important essay, in some ways at least as significant to the student of government as the essay *On Liberty.* But in connection with our concern with freedom in this lecture we have chosen *On Liberty* as of primary significance. In this essay John Stuart Mill faces, as I said a moment ago, the problem of the abuse of power outside government by forces in a pluralistic society. He states his primary objective on page seven of *On Liberty*'s Introductory section. "Like other tyrannies, the tyranny of the majority was at first and is still vulgarly held in dread, chiefly as operating through the acts of public authorities." It is this problem of the tyranny of the majority that concerns Mill. It is a problem that you know also turns up in the writings of de Tocqueville, an older friend of Mill's by whose thinking and writing Mill was deeply influenced. This question of the tyranny of the majority just mentioned actually is the problem of the tyranny of any non-governmental force in the society.

The problem is stated in another way in his essay, *On Liberty*, when Mill writes: "The object of the essay is to assert one very simple principle as entitled to govern absolutely the dealing of society with the individual in the way of compulsion and control. That principle is that the sole end for which mankind are warranted, individually or collectively, in interfering with the liberty of action of any of their number is self-protection. The only purpose for which power can be rightfully exercised over any member of a civilized community against his will is to prevent harm to others. His own good, either physical or moral, is not a sufficient warrant." What Mill is saying is that it is nobody's business how one organizes his own affairs. It is nobody's business to make one a good man. The business of others and of government is to prevent one man from doing harm to another. This is, you might say, the quintessence of radical individualism in terms of self-development. The development of the self is each self's sole responsibility and concerns no one else. This means, of course, the rejection of the entire Christian and Platonic tradition. Plato, as we shall see, is profoundly concerned with the betterment of men in society. Christianity, whether in St. Augustine or in any other Christian theorist, is profoundly concerned with the betterment of men in society according to some ideal notion of man. Society and government are seen as the corrective agency. To this proposition Mill says "no," it is nobody's job but man's to decide how he might become good. The key sentence here which you will want to mark on your own copy is on page 13. "Over himself, over his own body and mind, the individual is sovereign." The sovereignty of the individual is the heart and soul of this essay, *On Liberty*. This notion of the sovereignty of the individual is not wholly novel. The great German philosopher, Immanuel Kant, had been profoundly concerned with this very issue and his doctrine of the autonomy of the individual is the very heart of his doctrine of practical philosophy. I do not now have the time to elaborate the theme of his writings on ethics which is the categorical imperative, but those of you who are interested in philosophy ought to remind yourselves that this sentence, "over himself the individual is sovereign," makes sense only if it is implemented by the idea that this individual is motivated by a universal law as embodied in the categorical imperative.

Two other questions arise when one considers this doctrine of liberalism as expounded by Locke, Kant, Paine, Mill, and many others. One is the question of the decline of political liberalism, and the other is the question as to whether this decline marks the failure of liberalism.

The decline of political liberalism is a very striking thing in many places, more particularly in England, its original home. As you know, the Liberal Party gradually disintegrated and today, while still getting three million votes, it gets only a few seats in Parliament and plays a relatively insignificant role. What explains this decline of liberalism? The answer must be sought along lines which I indicated to you in my last lecture. It also has to do with the process of democratization. Mill is still in the aristocratic tradition of England throughout the entire essay of *On Liberty*. His concern is with the exceptional man. It is said by some that the essay was motivated by the fact that he thought it his own business whether or not he wanted to live with his girlfriend out of marriage. He did just this and people were scandalized. Mill thought it was no business of theirs whether he did or not. This is the human situation behind the writing of *On Liberty* which you have to bear in mind. The important point, however, is that as industrial capitalism unfolded in all its splendor and terror, the fate of an exceptional man and his love life became a rather less important problem to most people than the problem of the position of the ordinary man in this society. In other words, the problem of individual liberty receded as compared with the question of the effective participation in the political community and all that that implies.

In seeking to understand the decline of liberalism one should also remember that a good deal of what was relevant in liberalism has been absorbed into what goes under the name of social democracy. The English Labour Party carries a substantial heritage of English liberalism. This merger was made easier by John Stuart Mill himself, the John Stuart Mill of the *Political Economy*. If you read that much heavier and longer book, you will see that Mill works around by a very careful argument to a species of liberal socialism in the end. This path would be followed by other liberals like Hobhouse later in the century.

But liberalism has also spread to and in a very real sense conquered the conservative position. To be a conservative in England or America, must needs imply a substantial amount of liberalism; for the social order to be conserved is a liberal order. Not only in England, but on the Continent as well, "Liberal" parties in France, in Italy, in Germany are conservative parties, typically split to be sure, into a number of more or less liberal factions. It is a theme that was struck already by Edmund Burke in his "Appeal from the New to the Old Whigs" in which the conservative liberal speaks out against the views which to him seem to have led down the road to the French revolution. Friedrich Hayek's *Road to Serfdom* was a comparable reaction to the totalitarian revolution of our times.

One final question, then. Is liberalism really a failure? Is it "old hat" as some would assert today? My own inclination is to say "no." I think that there is certainly a historical aspect to liberalism which is clearly evident in many of the formulations you read in Locke and Mill. There is also, however, a timeless quality in liberalism which is its intrinsic humanism. When the totalitarians, more particularly the communist totalitarians, came along to challenge liberalism, they rightfully started by attacking what was conditioned by time and circumstance and linked to particular economic relationships. They ended up, however, by challenging the timeless element in liberalism and thereby challenged much more than liberalism. It is to this problem that I want to turn in my next two lectures.

READINGS, SUGGESTED AND REQUIRED

For General Reference:

S. I. BENN and R. S. PETERS, *The Principles of Political Thought* (The Free Press).

W. Y. ELLIOTT and N. A. MACDONALD, *Western Political Heritage* (Prentice-Hall).

C. J. FRIEDRICH, *Man and His Government: An Empirical Theory of Politics* (McGraw-Hill).

G. H. SABINE, *A History of Political Theory* (Holt).

Lectures 1 and 2:

REQUIRED READING:

JOHN LOCKE, *Second Treatise on Civil Government* (Library of Liberal Arts, Bobbs-Merrill).

J. S. MILL, "On Liberty" in *The Philosophy of J. S. Mill*, ed. Cohen (Modern Library).

JOHN PLAMENATZ, *Man and Society*, Vol. I, Ch. 6 (McGraw-Hill).

SUGGESTIONS FOR FURTHER READING:

CHRISTIAN BAY, *The Structure of Freedom* (Atheneum).

ISAIAH BERLIN, *Two Concepts of Freedom* (Oxford University Press).

MAURICE CRANSTON, *Freedom: A New Analysis* (Longmans, Green).

MAURICE CRANSTON, *John Locke* (Verry).

ERICH FROMM, *Escape from Freedom* (Avon).

JOSEPH HAMBURGER, *Intellectuals in Politics: John Stuart Mill and the Philosophic Radicals* (Yale).

LOUIS HARTZ, *Liberal Tradition in America* (Harcourt, Brace & World).

DAVID HUME, "Of the Original Contract," in *Political Essays* (Library of Liberal Arts, Bobbs-Merrill).

Liberty, ed. Friedrich, Nomos IV (Atherton Press).

JOHN LOCKE, *A Letter Concerning Toleration* (Library of Liberal Arts, Bobbs-Merrill).

J. S. MILL, "Utilitarianism," in *The Philosophy of J. S. Mill* (Modern Library).

The Philosophy of Kant, ed. Friedrich (Modern Library).

JOHN PLAMENATZ, *English Utilitarians* (Humanities Press).

The Political Theory of T. H. Green, ed. Rodman,

MELVIN RICHTER, *Politics of Conscience: T. H. Green and his Age* (Harvard).

3

Revolution and Social Justice

THE ORIGINAL POSITION of Western liberalism has been a revolutionary challenge to established tradition. In expounding the idea of freedom, it had challenged authority. Men were free to cultivate and perfect their selves, to maintain a private sphere of conviction and possession, to participate in public life, the shaping of laws and policies, and to innovate and create in both these spheres, and thereby to go beyond them into a future which transcends tradition, questions existing authority. In the course of time, liberalism became tame. It urged the value of free institutions, but maintained that these ought to be achieved gradually, ought to *evolve* through the "tactic of history"—in Burke's famous phrase. The French Revolution, started in the name of liberty, jeopardized its original thrust. In its course, social justice came to replace freedom as the basic challenge, and socialism was born. Thus social justice became the focal point of the succession of revolutions since that time. Social justice has, of course, always been a major concern of man. But it is a curious feature of social justice in Western history that it has rarely been analyzed by its ardent apostles. It has more or less been assumed as an obvious goal. This is due, of course, to its religious basis.

Sometimes its most urgent advocates have been the least explicit. In spite of his passionate concern with social justice, Karl Marx was rather inclined to talk about justice in deprecatory terms. Justice, in his opinion, was a bourgeois prejudice. If you look up Karl Marx's *Kapital,* particularly the first part, you will actually find only one explicit reference to justice. In the index of the 3 volumes justice appears only once. It is the citation for the first volume where Marx talks about the failure of justice in the bourgeois world in connection with a particular event in England, which incidentally is quite relevant today because it was a case of what we now would call urban renewal. Workers were thrown out of their slum quarters and nothing was done to provide for their living elsewhere. Marx contrasts this with the way in which a proprietor or businessman who loses his property is compensated not only for what the property is worth but also provided with a handsome profit. With an exclamation mark Marx says, "Look at what the bourgeois world calls justice!" Generally speaking then his argument is not cast in terms of justice. Despite this I believe that justice is the very heart of Marxist analysis. But today I am not going to talk about Marx in elucidating the concept of social justice, but rather about his antecedents. What I want to discuss is social justice and socialism in relation to the Western tradition of revolutionary development. You might actually call today's lecture one on social justice and revolution.

Social justice in terms of this discussion is not concerned with the great traditional discussion of justice—that I will take up later; rather the emphasis is on *social* justice. This aspect of justice is in common understanding taken to mean simply some kind of material well-being, i.e., equality of men with respect to material possessions and goods. (Later we shall take up the general problem of equality.) In this sense the idea of social justice has its roots in the Old and New Testament. In ancient Israel there was a provision for a kind of redistribution of wealth. Every so often all debts were abolished. This must have been a rather extraordinary arrangement for social life in Israel. It embodied, however, a very basic idea of the makers of ancient Israel and it became a key idea in the New Testament, not in this particular institutional form, but as a primary consideration in connection with society. The pursuit of social justice thus became an important element in the Judaeo-Christian tradition and persisted into the Middle Ages. In the great peasant revolts of the sixteenth century which spread through England, Bohemia, and Germany, vast revolutionary movements broke out, the purpose of which was to achieve social justice. Social justice for these peasants consisted primarily in greater economic well-being. An interesting institutional tradition lay behind these uprisings. In the primitive village community of the early Middle Ages, which goes even farther back into the tribal past of the Germanic peoples, there had been common property, more particularly of pasture and forest. This common property in pasture and forest was gradually usurped by the feudal lords and the subsequent dependency of the peasant on the feudal lords became increasingly burdensome. In all these peasant revolts the recapture of the common land, so basic to the village community's economic existence, was thus a very important ingredient. In this sense then the peasant revolts were really conservative, or indeed reactionary. They sought to re-establish an older tradition of social justice which had been put into jeopardy. They were also revolutionary, however, in the sense that they became associated with the efforts of the reformers, Wycliffe in England, Hus in Bohemia and Luther in Germany.

As a result of these unsuccessful endeavors to effect social change the idea of a revolutionary achievement of social justice continues to play a role in all subsequent revolutionary activities. In the English revolution, for example, though primarily conducted by the Puritans in the name of religious liberty and constitutional-ism, there sprang up a more radical group known as the Diggers who sought to achieve social justice by dint of seizing and culti-vating the land as a common possession of all. Actually, I've always considered the Diggers rather droll. They were a very small element in the Revolution, and played an insignificant role, never being in a position to challenge the dominant revolutionary forces under Cromwell. The Diggers were a small band of men who went to Richmond Hill, outside London, and there began to dig the soil. They claimed that the soil was common property and that the only salvation for man was to live on land that they had themselves dug. Gerrard Winstanley, their leader, remained a rather obscure man, but the doctrine had implications for the future.

In the later phases of the French Revolution the radical idea of social justice again asserted itself. It was particularly expounded by a man named Babeuf. He was very radical in his revolutionary outlook and point of view. Once again, however, he was unable to achieve ascendancy over the more dominant bourgeois elements who were the prime carriers of the revolutionary ferment.

In the nineteenth century this pursuit of social justice crystallized into a whole series of ideologies and ideologically cast doctrines, known as socialism. Socialism became a variegated creed, expounded by many thinkers in a variety of different ways. The foremost important ones were St. Simon, Owen, Fourier and Proudhon, three Frenchmen and one Englishman. They all shared a violent hostility towards private property which was put in the most dramatic form by Proudhon, who wrote that "property is theft." This is the group of writers Marx attacks in the *Communist Manifesto* as Utopian Socialists, simple minded seekers after social justice blind to the scientific laws of history. The interesting thing is that although these Utopian Socialists elaborated their different ideas on a future society and how this society might be achieved they never particularly elaborated on the content of their notion of social justice. It always contained, as I said, some idea of radical egalitarianism. Material goods ought to be equally or more equally distributed. Beyond that, however, the analysis lacked specificity. As I already indicated, even in Marx and Engels, social justice did not really receive any further explication. Yet it was quite widely appreciated by these thinkers and writers that the elimination of private property from the social fabric was a radical revolutionary enterprise calling for a complete transformation of the society. This leads me to turn to the problem and the concept of revolution.

I don't know whether you have ever had occasion to reflect upon the fact that the attitude to revolution found in our Western society is quite distinctive and quite different from that of other political societies and civilizations. It is different because it is a semi-positive attitude, based on an appreciation of the function of social change and revolution. If you read the thinkers of classical antiquity, Plato, Aristotle and Polybius, you find them all concerned with how to avoid change. They all are concerned with how to stop and prevent revolution. In our modern West there may still be a good deal of anti-revolutionary sentiment. As you know much recent American legislation such as the Smith Act is to some extent concerned with this problem of how to prevent a violent overthrow of the established order of things. Nevertheless, the attitude of the West is generally favorable to change. The point of view and position is that revolutions are usually good things. Jefferson has a famous line about how "the tree of liberty must be refreshed from time to time with the blood of patriots and tyrants,—its natural manure." Such a call to revolutionary violence may sound strange to the ears of contemporary Americans; but it is an integral part of the American ideology. Abe Lincoln, another great molder of our American tradition, made similar statements several times and I shall analyze one below. Revolution is thus accepted as part of the ordinary fabric of society. Of course the American nation itself was born in revolutionary upheaval. To be sure, it has become popular in recent years, following de Tocqueville, to claim that America's birth was not a result of revolution. It has even been proclaimed as one of the great discoveries of de Tocqueville, that America is different from Europe because it hasn't known a revolution. Personally, I am rather skeptical about this alleged insight of de Tocqueville. I think that the American Revolution was to all intents and purposes very much a revolution. It was certainly thought to be so in London. In view of what has been happening all over the world in recent years which we speak of as the colonial revolution, I think it is a mistake not to recognize that this particular effort in 1776 of a group of colonial people to make themselves independent was a revolution. It was certainly a different kind of revolution from that which occurred several years later in France; but it was, nonetheless, a revolution. For this reason I think that one is still justified in saying that at the beginning of the American commonwealth a revolution stands as the primary creative act. Even if you want to leave America aside, this is certainly true of France. The entire history of modern France is shaped by the great revolution that occurred in France shortly after the American Revolution. The same thing is true of the contemporary Soviet Union. It is also true of contemporary Germany and contemporary Italy. Nearly everywhere revolutions have been the creative commencement of a political order and a political society.

The relevance and significance for most societies of an actual revolutionary experience has helped create that curious attitude of Western man which inclines him to think of revolutions as something not wholly bad. This is also connected with the fact, which I have already hinted at, that Western man is inclined to think of change as a good thing. The great Heraclitus said at the beginning of Greek philosophy, *panta rei*—all is in flux. This he suggested as the true insight into the nature of things. Modern man of the West has accepted this insight and gone even farther in assuming that flux is good. Therefore a good political order is a political order that provides for change, not a political order that prevents change. We are inclined to prefer our constitutional system, because it is a system that allows for change to occur regularly and without the necessity of revolutionary excesses. Over the course of time, however, we can still say that revolution has occurred in America, not only the Industrial Revolution, but other kinds of important changes. For this reason I think it has been said with some justice that American history is an organized revolution in permanence. On this score I think that there is very little doubt that from the point of view of Europe one of the things that is considered either very good or very bad about America is that it has continually revolutionized Western society in the course of its existence. Within the context of Western culture, America has been the revolutionary force par excellence. It has continually provided stimulus for change and sometimes radical change.

In this connection, I think it quite interesting to reflect upon how European history has in a sense been shaped by great revolutions. I would call to your attention that there is a difference between what we tend to call the great revolutions, and what you might call the more ordinary and regular revolutions of a political sort. When Aristotle talks about revolutions he is thinking of the latter kind. We might call them limited revolutions, that is to say, revolutions in which the primary focus is on the change of government, on the change of the political order. The great revolutions involve more than simply this. They bring about a far-reaching transformation in all aspects of man's life. Our model great revolution is the French Revolution, but it is equally true of the English Revolution and the German Revolution which we call the Reformation. In each of these great revolutions the change in the political order seems almost incidental to other and more basic changes which suddenly break forth in the particular society, and threaten to alter it fundamentally in virtually every respect, culturally, economically, socially and politically.

We all think now in terms of comparative civilizations, under the influence of such thinkers as Toynbee and Spengler. As compared with other civilizations, it is characteristic of Western society that it should have had its history shaped by a succession of great revolutions. Each one of these revolutions broke out in a particular nation, and each of these revolutions had a special significance for that particular nation. Indeed, one very imaginative philosopher of history, Rosenstock-Hussy, has insisted that the nations were shaped by their particular revolutions. The Germans were formed by the Reformation, the English by the revolution of the seventeenth century, and the French by their revolution at the end of the eighteenth century. Even if one doesn't carry the analysis that far, it is very clear that such a succession of revolutions is not found in non-western histories. Look at the history of India, the history of China, or the history of other great civilizations like the civilization of classical antiquity. They are not marked by these dramatic turns, these cataclysmic alterations in cultural, social, economic and political affairs which these revolutions marked for the Western world. A word of caution is perhaps appropriate here. Because of the significance of revolution in our own particular historical context, some people think of all revolutionary activity as somehow expressing thrusts that have the significance of great revolutions. This is a mistake. I think it is necessary not to overlook the limited revolution which is primarily political in scope and purpose. This kind of political revolution does occur and has its own intrinsic dynamic.

I think it necessary to realize that at the heart of each of these great revolutions and at the present time even of some of the not-so-great revolutions, is the idea of social justice. You might say that this concern for social justice is the core of the revolution's ideology and that ideological aspects are the characteristic features of the modern revolution. You find nothing of this ideological aspect in Aristotle. For Aristotle, revolutions revolved around the perpetual struggle between the rich and the poor. Of course you can say that the struggle between the rich and the poor is an argument about social justice. In a sense it would be difficult to deny this. But the interesting thing is that the attitude of Aristotle toward the struggling participants is a totally different one from modern writers. He does not think that because the argument in the revolution is between the rich and the poor you must therefore say that the poor are in the right because the poor are seeking social justice. This is not Aristotle's view at all. As far as Aristotle is concerned the argument of social justice is irrelevant. The tendency of Aristotle is to say "a plague on both your houses." The argument on grounds of social justice is a bad one. A good society is one in which this argument plays no role. Thus we can better understand Aristotle's emphasis on the middle class. The predominance of the middle class prevents that bifurcation of society into rich and poor and hence avoids that instability which in turn leads to revolution.

In the modern age, however, and throughout the whole development of the revolutionary propensity of Western society, the notion has been that the revolution produces some thing in the way of an approximation to a better state of society. It is conceded that there are all kinds of unpleasant aspects to revolution. Violence always accompanies revolution and this is a bad thing. There are many other things that one does not approve of in revolutions; but in the end one must admit that revolutions are worthwhile. So the argument runs; revolutions mark a forward step in the evolution of society and their bad features must be condoned because of their contribution to the achievement of progress toward a more perfect society.

There is a rather interesting point connected with these so-called bad features of revolution which I would like to elaborate for you a bit. There seems to be a definite succession of phases or stages in a revolutionary development. The first phase or stage is one in which the existing order of things develops an increasing amount of tensions, break-downs, an increasing amount that is of uncertainties, which in political terms mean that the legitimacy of the rulers is becoming more and more dubious and their authority declines. In other words, government becomes weaker as it fails to satisfy those subject to its rule. Parallel to this weakening of the government, various movements spring up, usually among intellectuals and discontented elements in the population. These groups argue that an alteration must take place, and that a new kind of order must be created. As these movements develop, they become filled with idealistic zeal and a readiness for sacrifice. At a certain point this readiness for sacrifice becomes so great and the idealistic fervor so pronounced that the revolutionary outbreak occurs. Lo and behold, usually to the surprise of everybody, structures collapse which had until that time seemed very durable and powers fall which had hitherto seemed very effective and indeed fierce. Overnight they reveal themselves as the hollow façade that they had become during the process of disintegration. The revolutionary movement then installs itself in the seats of power and is soon confronted with the complete tasks of operating the society. This turns out to be a very much more arduous task than the revolutionaries had imagined in their enthusiasm. They find themselves faced with all kinds of detail which is very difficult to manipulate. The more concrete the idealism of the revolutionaries, the more specific their purposes and intentions with reference to the new society being created, the greater are these difficulties. It now turns out that to create a wholly new political and social order involves an infinite variety of political operations. and therefore a great variety of human beings, both savory and unsavory, to perform the necessary tasks. Crane Brinton has pointed out in his *Anatomy of Revolution,* a book in which this entire revolutionary process is very skilfully analyzed, that a revolution, like any other scheme of politics, require all kinds of people. It requires clever people and a lot of dumb people; it requires heroes, martyrs and crooks. All kinds of persons can be found in the revolution and this of course creates once again the typical problems of government and politics.

As this becomes clear, two things happen. On the one hand, disillusionment sets in among those who had been members of the revolutionary movement. On the other hand, the revolutionary rulers use more and more violence when they discover that their rule may be endangered. Hence the propensity towards the development of terror in the later phases of a revolutionary enterprise. This terror gets out of hand and at the same time the tasks which the revolution originally intended to accomplish remain unfulfilled. This usually leads to a reaction which in accordance with the model of the French Revolution is known as the Thermidorian Reaction. The "thermidor," meaning the month of July-August in the revolutionary calendar, is the point at which the revolutionary enterprise turns into a kind of reaction. I don't think it is truly a reaction; it is more an abandonment of the revolutionary purposes. But the Thermidorian Reaction in turn dissatisfies, displeases, and finally loses what little legitimacy it had. So in the final phase, the revolution is followed by a dictatorship which in turn is overthrown by a restorative effort at reproducing the condition that existed before the revolution. The old order cannot, of course, be reproduced; it cannot be restored. Thus the society settles down to the new state which the revolutionary dynamic has produced.

This is a very rough sketch of a pattern which has been observed time and again in the unfolding of these great revolutions and which appears to be an indication of inner laws of political and social change. One of the interesting, and in some ways striking features of the revolution in the Soviet Union was that the people who made that revolution were aware of the sequence of which I have spoken, and were therefore determined to prevent its recurrence. The Soviet doctrine of the Revolution in Permanence is part of that endeavor. An argument has been going on ever since the Revolution between outside observers and inside defenders of the Russian Revolution. Outside observers are inclined to claim that the same sequence has occurred, and the same results have been achieved. The insiders answer that the evolution in the Soviet Union has been all different. Stalin is not Napoleon and there is no Napoleon in sight and other arguments of this kind are urged. But the parallel need not be that specific, and some lines of Soviet development in recent years do fit the pattern.

Now one might ask how it had happened that Western society developed such a very different attitude toward revolution and therefore became if not enamored of revolution, then at least ready to accept revolution as the inevitable consequence of societal evolution. A statement by Lincoln may help here. In speaking on the Mexican War (and it was a situation not too different from the ones we are confronting now) he said in Congress on January 12, 1848: "Any people anywhere being inclined and having the power, have the right to rise up and shake off the existing government, and form a new one that suits them better. This is a most valuable, a most sacred right . . . More than this, a majority of any portion of such people may revolutionize, putting down a minority . . ." And as if to make doubly sure that his meaning be taken in the radical sense of an overthrow of established institutions, he added: "It is a quality of revolutions not to go by old ideas or old laws . . ." What this means is that behind all positive laws and constitutions, there exists a higher law expressed in a people's rights as human beings. This right is definitely linked with the doctrine of human rights and the related notion of a right of revolution.

If you trace the theory of a right of revolution back you find its first explicit enunciation is generally believed to have been offered in Locke's famous *Second Treatise on Civil Government* where he presumably defends the Revolution of 1688. Curiously enough the Revolution of 1688, the so-called "glorious revolution," was neither "glorious" nor a "revolution." It was essentially a *coup d'État* executed with great skill but with a significant lack of any human characteristic that could be described as glorious. Locke's *Treatise* spoke in terms, however, more general than simply of 1688. Indeed recent historical research has discovered that this essay was not written for the defense of the Revolution of 1688, but that it was composed quite a few years before in defense of a revolution yet to come. England, of course, had had a great Revolution in the middle of the century. Surely in the great Puritan revolution there can be found an ideologue who discovered and described the intrinsic right to a revolutionary enterprise. There was such a thinker, none other than the great John Milton, poet and propagandist of Oliver Cromwell.

John Milton, in his famous defense of the Revolution of 1647–48, for the first time actually enunciated quite explicitly the right of revolution, the right of a people to arrange their government as they pleased. It is interesting that this occurs, not by itself, but within the context of an argument of the right of resistance. In a sense Milton's propaganda pamphlet is the last in a whole series of writings on the right of resistance and the first in enunciating the right of revolution. What had been the situation before that time? It had always been argued in the Reformation and in the Middle Ages that people had a right of resistance against tyrants. By tyrants were understood rulers who violated the law, and did not obey the principles which underlay their institution. This notion of the subjection of rulers to law can be traced back to the Old Testament where the priests and the prophets had repeatedly reminded the rulers that they must obey the law if they were to continue in power. This tradition of the right of resistance against an unlawful and tyrannical ruler is connected with the scriptural saying that man must obey God more than other men. This in a sense is the Judaeo-Christian root of the favorable attitude to revolution. The argument is found in a great many different variations. If, for example, a ruler breaks the law, it is argued that he does something contrary to the will of God, and since people must obey the will of God, they must disobey such a ruler and resist him. This traditional argument exhibits a great many different shadings as to how much resistance is allowed. There are many different opinions on whether one can kill a tyrant or just restrain him. If restraint then who can restrain him? All of these ideas are part of a great tradition that culminates in Milton who, after reproducing all of the arguments about the right of resistance, suddenly proclaims in a most memorable passage which has not been given sufficient attention that even if the ruler should not be a tyrant, a people can do away with him simply because it is the God-given right of every people to give itself the form of government it likes.

Thus in his *Tenure of Kings and Magistrates,* John Milton proclaimed that "all men were naturally born free," that they were "born to command and not to obey," and that "since the king or magistrate holds his authority of the people," the people "may, as oft as they shall judge it for the best, either choose him or reject him, retain him or depose him, *though no tyrant,* merely by the liberty and right of free-born men to be governed as seems to them best." Otherwise, the "government, though not illegal, or intolerable, hangs over them as a lordly scourge, not as a free government"; and "therefore to be abrogated." For, and this is the final point "justice is the only true sovereign and supreme majesty upon earth." Here you have an unabashed proclamation of the right of revolution. It is no longer a question of whether the ruler is tyrannical or not, whether he is unlawful or not. It is simply a question of what the people want. If the people no longer like what they have in the way of government, or political order, they can do away with it and put another in its place. At this point no idea of social justice intervenes, except in so far as the people's preferences embody it.

It is very interesting that if you go to the document in which is found the crucial doctrine of the American revolutionary enterprise, namely, the Declaration of Independence, you find there this characteristic combination of particular grievances and the unfettered, universal principle of popular sovereignty. On the one hand there is a proclamation of the God-given right of people to determine for themselves how they wish to be governed. On the other hand, in the latter part of the Declaration, which nobody ever reads, there is a long recital of all the misdeeds of George III, the tyrant in London who must be overthrown. This is a combination of these two traditions of resistance and revolution. There is here the argument that the ruler is a tyrant, and therefore he may be overthrown. This argument is inconclusive as far as the American Revolution is concerned because the colonists never proposed to depose George III. They were quite willing to let the British live under this tyrant if they should so choose. But there is the other aspect: the general right of revolution. All the Americans proposed to do was say that "we the American people have the right to give ourselves our own form of government." In a sense, you might say that it is this which is at the heart of the tradition of Western revolution. This tradition sees revolution as a vital link of an outworn past with a promising future. It is the heir of the eschatological hopes of the biblical tradition: the chosen people who shall inherit the earth, and the belief in a paradise of perfect justice to come. How Karl Marx and his followers adapted this tradition to their world revolutionary purpose will be the subject of the next lecture. Theirs was and is a challenge to the entire Western heritage, and not only that of Liberalism.

4

Marx, Marxism and the

Totalitarian Challenge

WE TURN TODAY TO KARL MARX, the greatest of the philosophers of socialism. Karl Marx himself was a humanist and a passionate believer in social justice. Indeed there is something of the Old Testament prophet about the approach of Karl Marx. Although himself convinced of the strictly scientific nature of his insights, they actually were inspired by deep emotion and passionate concern. Although you may not have thought so, the ideas of Karl Marx have played a great role in the development of the notion of social justice. The way in which he systematized and transcended the tradition of socialism and social justice has had a profound and catastrophic effect upon the development of Western society and mankind. The Marxist political outlook, as it developed, became not merely a challenge to liberalism, but to the entire Western heritage of political thought. It was not so understood by Marx himself, who saw his approach rather as a fulfillment of that heritage.

In what follows, I shall not so much deal with the challenge as such. For it is quite clearly implied in what I wish to discuss with you, namely the main elements in Marx' and Engels' political thought. Beginning with Marx's notion of the state and its withering away, and the related Janus-faced image of man, I shall briefly take up in turn his theory of alienation, Marx's dynamic materialism as implied in the theory that the primary given in the forward march of civilization is the control of the means of production. In turn I shall deal with the doctrine of class struggle as the core of history, the resulting dialectical materialism, and the related notions of the superstructure and of ideology. Returning to the Marxian notion of the state and its "withering away," the ideas on the revolution and more particularly the dictatorship of the proletariat, I shall finally deal with its totalitarian implications, the Fascist reaction and the imperialist trend in both Communism and Fascism.

The fascinating and central feature of Marx's challenge to liberalism, and indeed to the Western heritage, is his extraordinary combination of radical moral dogmatism expressed in his fervent belief in social justice with a profound conviction of the scientific nature of the social analysis. Upon such analysis both the program of political action and the prediction of the future are based; to sum it up: "freedom flowers in necessity." Revolutions were seen by Marx dialectically as the same manifestation of man's ultimate political freedom as is displayed in the activity of the individual in his social and political life. Hence, one finds in Marx the very curious, and from a logical point of view perplexing contradiction between what the historical necessities have decreed and what the individual is called upon to do. The objection that this is a basic contradiction is transcended in Marxism by the acceptance of contradiction as inescapable, as part of the human condition. Social justice is in a sense the key to this contradiction. There is a continual evolution in society. Values, means of production, techniques, and the beliefs associated with all these things are continually evolving and call for continuous adjustment if social justice is to be achieved. These adjustments finally culminate in the consummation of the Communist Revolution.

Marx states in the *Communist Manifesto,* which still is in many ways the best and the most condensed dramatic statement of his political position, that the other socialists who preceded him were Utopians. He saw his doctrine as supplanting the Utopians by eliminating their deficiencies. What made Marx think that his analysis was not Utopian, but practical and realistic was his belief that he had discovered the reality of power and the reality of the state in which power was organized. Unlike his Utopian predecessors, he was convinced that the only way Communism could be achieved would be through the overthrow of the established political order, the destruction of the state. For the state, for Marx, is "the executive committee of the ruling class."

This destruction of the state is, in a way, rather different from what nowadays is often associated in the minds of people in the United States and elsewhere with the notion of socialism. The common notion of socialism is that it is every kind of doctrine which looks upon the state as saviour, which wants to turn over everything to the state. You encounter this attitude practically any time you suggest that some particular ill should be taken care of by the state. Someone who doesn't agree with you is apt to say: "Well, you are a socialist." The notion prevails that socialism is a kind of doctrine which looks to the state as the panacea, the solution to all problems. This, however, is far from the solution of Marx. To Marx the state was not the solution to all things; on the contrary, the state is the hard core of the enemy which must be destroyed.

What is going to happen after the state, which is the agent of the enemy class, has been conquered and its power seized by the revolutionaries? The answer which Marx and the Marxists give is that the state will die, or, as the rather erroneous translation which has become accepted in English has it, the state will wither away. The German word is really *"absterben"* which means "die," not wither away. This withering away of the state which has been conquered by the revolutionary force occurs in connection with the creation of the new society. I shall come back to this a little later.

There is, however, an intermediary stage between the conquest of state power by the revolutionaries and the dying away of the state after the consummation of the revolution. This is the stage of the dictatorship of the proletariat. At this stage all the various remaining elements in the previous order of society, more particularly capitalism, will be destroyed. When that has been accomplished, there is no longer any need of the state. At this point the stateless society of the paradisaical future can commence.

This rather dramatic notion of a transformation of a society through revolutionary action reveals Marxist thinking revolving around two divergent notions of man. The nature of man after the revolution is consummated is radically different from the nature of man before the revolution occurred. In the age of pre-revolution capitalism with which Marx was primarily concerned, man's nature was viewed in a rather pessimistic light, very much along the lines of Hobbes and the Hobbesians. Man is greedy, egotistic, aggressive, immoral, and so forth and so on. These are all drawn together in the belief that pre-revolutionary man is not free, but is subject to the determination of social forces over which he has no control. This deterministic and negative image of man is itself part of the Christian tradition, which after all sees man in terms of the doctrine of "original sin," that is as a rather hopeless and despicable being who can only be rescued by the infinite grace of the Deity. In Marx's thought you have, in a way, the retention of this Christian idea. Instead of the grace of the Deity rescuing man from his evil nature you have the spirit of the revolution which is going to accomplish this radical transformation.

After this change has been consummated man's nature, suggests Marx, is no longer as Hobbes described it but as Rousseau did in his most optimistic and romantic passages. The human being is now cooperative, loving, neighborly and ready to share his goods with others. He is willing to accept the needs of others as the essential guide for his actions. Lest you think I am telling you a fairy tale about Marx's Rousseauistic conception of man, it should be noted that Engels himself has quite explicitly stated that Marxism is a modification and elaboration of Rousseau's

Essay on Inequality, the essay in which this point of view is particularly and dramatically insisted on by Rousseau. Inequality, the Marxist and Rousseau would suggest, was the creation of civilization and more particularly of private property and what is needed is a return to the kind of conditions which existed before civilization was created. This is precisely the kind of condition to which the revolution will lead.

It is most interesting that in the newest explicit statement of the Marxist position, namely in the new program of the Communist Party of the Soviet Union, these positions are repeated in their essential form. The New Program states in its Introduction that the supreme goal of the Party is to build a communist society on whose banner will be inscribed: "From each according to his abilities, to each according to his needs. Everything for the sake of man and for the benefit of man." This is exactly the formulation—if you read the *Communist Manifesto* you will see it—in which this whole position culminates "to each according to his needs, from each according to his ability." In other words, distribution of goods is no longer related to achievement. It is related to need. Everyone is going to be happy to contribute his ability whether superior or not to society for the benefit of his neighbor. Marx and Engels built this kind of modernized Rousseauism on the work of a nineteenth-century American anthropologist, Louis Morgan, who claimed on the basis of his research that there had been a golden age of communal harmony in which there had been no property, no exploitation, no classes and no slaves. These claims of Morgan are today considered extremely questionable and the criticism of them has played an important part in stimulating the development of modern anthropology. This notwithstanding, one of the recent commentaries on the Marx-Engels' version of Morgan would have it that "the early, primitive society is seen as a spontaneously integrated society with a real general will." In other words, the contention is that what Rousseau talked about was something which did exist at one time before the advent of the civilizing forces of modern capitalism and indeed before the societal stages which led to capitalism.

There turns up in this connection a doctrine which has in recent years become very much talked about and which no doubt you yourselves have encountered. This is the doctrine of alienation. Marx and Engels believed that men have become alienated from themselves and their work. Already in his *Critique of the Hegelian Philosophy of Law* in 1844 Marx struck the keynote of this idea when he wrote: "A critique of religion leads to the doctrine that the highest being for man is man himself, hence to the categorical imperative to overthrow all relationships in which man is humbled, enslaved, abandoned, despised." He later made the point more specific, relating the notion of alienation more specifically to man's work and his feeling about it. There is at present a trend to generalize the notion once more in psychological terms which are reminiscent of Hegel. But this kind of alienation is not what Marx was talking about. Contemporary feeling is something much more nearly found in Hegel than in Marx. For it is a psychological and spiritual phenomenon in the sense of a man being separated from genuine community and being separated from the corresponding inner life. This notion does occur in the early Marx while he was still very much under the influence of Hegel. But Marx later transformed alienation into more of an economic category. In *Das Kapital*, alienation means essentially that human beings have been alienated from the product of their work. Indeed labor has become a commodity like any other. Work is thus transformed into a physical thing which people buy without ever thinking of the human beings that are involved. The buyers of merchandise no longer think of the men who created it. Men have become alienated, Marx suggests, in the sense of having become materially estranged from what they originally were. This is of course a subtler notion and in many ways quite different from the psychological notion which Hegel developed. Alienation in Hegel is connected with culture growth and man becoming estranged from his true self. In this connection Hegel introduced the famous opposition of master and servant (not slave, as is sometimes said). I must remind you of this theory; for the discussion of master and servant in Hegel was important in influencing Marx's own thinking and development. But in Hegel the world, history, indeed all reality was seen in terms of spiritual forces and spiritual problems. Marx, being the determined materialist that he was and wanted to be, prided himself on having turned things right side up again that Hegel had turned upside down, as he puts it in the introduction to *Das Kapital*. In Marx's notions, then, it was not the spiritual but the material that was the crucial aspect of reality. At this point it is necessary, however, to recall that materialism for Marx was a more specific and subtler notion than older elementary materialism which Marx himself calls crude materialism. What Marx is really concerned with when he speaks of materialism in the social and political realm, is the control of the means of production. This *control* of the means of production, rather than the material means themselves, constituted the core of materialism in the societal realm. Now "control" is not quite a material thing. Control is something which involves human beings, human wills and human efforts. In that sense control is already in some respect removed from the strictly material. In this connection it is quite important to consider the concept of nature which is involved in this materialism. We know from one very important passage in Engels that materialism in a sense means to Marx, naturalism. It occurs in one of the more recondite bits dealing with "Ludwig Feuerbach and the end of classical German philosophy." This is what Engels wrote: "The answers which the philosophers gave to this question (namely the question did God create the world, or is the world in existence eternally) split them into two great camps. Those who asserted the primacy of spirit to nature, and therefore in the last instance assumed world-creation in some form or another, comprised the camp of idealism. The others who regarded nature as primary, belong to the various schools of materialism." Materialism is seen here as based on "natural" and hence as sound. The view has persisted in Marxism.

There is one interesting passage in the new program of the Communist Party of the Soviet Union in connection with the controversy over idealism and materialism. At the very start of the

Introduction where the program describes the beginnings of communism, it reads: "More than a hundred years ago Karl Marx and Friedrich Engels, the great teachers of the proletariat, wrote in the *Communist Manifesto,* 'a spectre is haunting Europe, the spectre of Communism.'" The Introduction goes on and states, "first dozens and hundreds of people, and then thousands and millions inspired by the *ideals* of communism, stormed the old world." This presumably scientific analysis of given conditions suddenly reveals itself as nonetheless containing an ideal. Indeed the implication is that this ideal was the real moving force. In terms of classical Marxism, it should not have read "inspired by the *ideals* of communism," but "convinced by the scientific analysis of Marx." The introduction to the new party program does, however, use "inspired by the ideals," which shows that they have not quite stayed with Engels and his juxtaposition of idealism and naturalism. Even so there can be very little doubt that materialism for Marx and Engels had essentially a very broad meaning because the meaning of naturalism is obviously a more comprehensive one than that of materialism.

Building on what has so far been analyzed, Marx and Engels proceeded to construct their famous pattern of historical development in terms of class struggle, relating it dialectically to inner contradictions. I am afraid that at this point I must bother you just a little with considering Hegel, trying as it is. For one must get a glimpse of the "dialectic." What really happened here—and it is a very dubious gloss on Hegel, I might say in passing—is that Marx simplified a crucial point in the analysis of the human mind that you find in Hegel's *Logic*. Hegel developed the notion that thinking is a dynamic process proceeding in terms of contradiction from thesis to antithesis to synthesis. "Being," "non-being" and "becoming" constitute the great triad with which Hegel begins his *Logic*. "Being" immediately posits "non-being" because one can not think of "being" without thinking also "non-being." Yet they contradict each other. If confronted with this contradiction of "being" and "non-being," what is one to do? The resolution, suggests Hegel, is "becoming," which is at the same time both "being" and "non-being" as one state continually passes into the next. This dialectical process is developed for other basic categories. This passing is a matter of transcending, superseding and yet also preserving the antecedent state. Hegel used for this process the German word "aufheben" which has the three distinct meanings of transcending, superseding and preserving all of which Hegel meant to imply when he employed it for describing the transition from thesis to antithesis to synthesis. Hegel, with his predominantly spiritual outlook, posited that this analysis of the human mind's processes was the key to an understanding of nature and of human history. This philosophy has had much greater influence, incidentally, as an interpretation of human history than it has of nature. But in any case, it treated real things in analogy to intellectual processes. Hegel's argument was fundamentally this: "The mind is part of the cosmos. If we can observe these intellectual processes in our mind we have a right to assume that they reveal the laws of the cosmos." This is the argument of which Marx says that it puts things upside down because it imputes to matter something that is characteristic of the mind. Marx feels that he is putting things right side up by making it clear that it is in material things that this dialectical process is buried which then is projected onto the mind.

At this point Marx introduces the notion of sequence in history, of successive stages dominated by successive means of production and their control exercised by successive classes. This is the famous doctrine of the pattern of history as the history of class struggles in which each successive class supersedes the preceding class because with the emergence of new means of production a different class is needed for handling these means of production. This is the heart of so-called dialectical materialism. I am pulling two things together here. If you make a really precise analysis of Marxism you must distinguish between dialectical materialism and historical materialism. I am putting these two things together, however, as indeed they are placed in the *Communist Manifesto*. Marx and Engels propose in the *Manifesto* that this dialectical process is intrinsically and inherently necessary and that it occurs as a result of laws of history which eventually culminate in the take-over by the last of these classes, the proletariat. This class is for the first time, say Marx and Engels proudly, the majority class. All other ruling classes have been minorities. Because the proletariat is the majority and eventually the overwhelming majority, it does not need force any more to accomplish its objectives; it can do everything on the basis of cooperative effort as I was just now explaining to you.

At this point we can turn to the next important category of Marxist thought, the superstructure. Religion, philosophy, art, literature, ethics and law are interpreted by Marx as mere ideology, mere superstructure. They have no independent meaning or significance except in terms of their justification of the position of a particular dominant class. Just as the state is interpreted as the executive committee of the dominant class, so philosophy and religion are part of the ideology of the dominant class. All spiritual and intellectual values dissolve into ideology, mere rationalizations of the interests of the dominant class. It thus becomes clear that Marxism is much more than simply a challenge to liberalism. It challenges the entire tradition of rationalism since the days of the Greeks. It challenges not only Western rationalism, but, also, for example, Indian intellectualism or Chinese intellectualism. All of these great cultures have over the last three or four thousand years developed elaborate structures of ideating analysis of truth by which they sought to understand reality. Marx says that all this is unrelated to reality, except through being a maid-servant to the power structure of the dominant class. What you must really do then is analyze the class structure to get the true meaning of such ideologies. This is what is generally spoken of as Marx's critique of ideology. In the last generation, however, one convinced Marxist, Karl Mannheim, a man of great intellectual power, began to be concerned about the implications of what was bound to come to light the moment the Communists took over a country like Russia when Marxism itself became a justification for the power of a particular group controlling a particular political order, in this case the Communist Party of the Soviet Union. This is actually the theme of Mannheim's famous work on *Ideology and Utopia* in which he tries to come to terms with the fact that this Marxist analysis is itself such an ideology.

This analysis of ideology leads into the Marxist doctrine of the "dictatorship of the proletariat." That in turn brings us back to what I said in my last lecture about the several phases in the revolutionary effort. Abbreviating and contracting it, one might say that there is first the phase of the revolutionary take-over followed by the phase of the dictatorship of the proletariat and consummated in the final phase of the dying-away of the state. Here again we face a dialectical triad. But there is very little doubt that Marx, and Engels, and for that matter many Marxists after them, did not consider either the first or the second phase as of any considerable duration. The revolutionary take-over would be a dramatic, violent event. When power had been seized and the revolutionaries were in charge, the dictatorship of the proletariat, essentially a dictatorship by the Communists on behalf of the proletariat, would make short shrift of the existing social and political organization and would create in its place the stateless society of the third phase. The growing prolongation of the assumed short second phase of the dictatorship of the proletariat has been the dominant development of the twentieth century. It is this dictatorship of the proletariat which has justifiably been spoken of as the "revolution in permanence." What the people who conquered state power in the Soviet Union discovered when they tackled the job of the dictatorship of the proletariat was that it was a much bigger and longer job than they had envisaged. It was a job that involved a much greater deployment of power than had been anticipated. If you read Marx, even in the later *Critique of the Gotha Program* wherein he is much more elaborate than in the *Communist Manifesto* about this undertaking, or Lenin's remarks in *State and Revolution,* it is fairly obvious that they both thought of state power as something that you merely took hold of the way I take hold of this desk. You take it and it is yours, and then you simply deploy it. There is in their views very little appreciation for the fluidity of power, that is to say for the fact that power is something which only exists in the exercise. They failed to appreciate that if you take over power what it really means is that you have only destroyed the power of one set of power wielders and that then you have to build your own power. Power is not simply yours through revolution because power exists in what men do in exercising their power. You must therefore do more than merely depose the powerholder and seize his power. You must, as Plato, Aristotle, and Machiavelli said, "build a state." You must create a political order. This is what the Communists unknowingly stumbled into; and this is what must, in my opinion, be borne in mind when one speaks of totalitarianism. It is simply not correct to assert that the Communists, when they made their revolution in 1917, intended to erect a totalitarian dictatorship. On the contrary, they thought they had come to create the conditions for a perfect anarchic democracy. In a brief intermediary period of construction they expected to eliminate completely what had hitherto been the power of the state. But as they tackled the job of building a new political order they found that task to be an extremely difficult one, particularly as they came to associate it in the Soviet Union with an economic revolution by which they wanted through a centralized planned effort to transform a society of peasants into an industrial civilization.

Having mentioned the transformation of a society in terms of its industrialization brings into view another element in the Marxian analysis. Something very important to bear in mind when talking of Marx, is to note that he thought that in terms of class analysis, the revolutionary effort would come in the last stages of industrial capitalism. It would come at that point when a vast mass of atomized and exploited workers confronted a few extremely rich and powerful men who exploited and dominated them. This mass of workers which contained the class-conscious elite of the communists would decide to do away with their exploiters and to step into their place. Now, as you know, nothing of the kind has happened. The countries that have gone forward in the process of industrial capitalism have developed social welfare and trade union policies which have brought about solutions for particular grievances. The capitalist societies have thus by no means produced the kind of situation which Marx envisaged. Instead of that, the Marxist kind of revolution has in fact occurred in agrarian societies, Russia and China, even Poland, Hungary, Rumania and Cuba. But since the image of the communist order called for an industrial society, all of these agrarian societies were at once confronted with the task of bringing about what in the original prediction already existed. This undertaking has become the primary task for the dictatorship of the proletariat. It is of course a task which requires considerable time. In connection with this effort features of the totalitarian dictatorship are worked out. Interestingly enough, and in spite of what has happened, the Communist Party program of 1961 still retains the old analysis. It suggests that after this transitional process is completed, there will arrive the day of paradisaical conditions which the original *Communist Manifesto* predicted. Indeed, some of the dramatic efforts that Khrushchev made in his day were part of an attempt to get a little bit closer to this kind of idyllic cooperative community.

There are two more points to make. The first is a word about Fascism. Fascism is by no means the equivalent of Communism, either intellectually, or in terms of its social thrust. You might say that Fascism is a reaction to Communism. It reacted to the political doctrine which I have just portrayed for you which the revolutionary Communists made their own. As a reaction to Communism Fascism was not included in the Marxist prophecy. This is a rather curious oversight and it suggests some of the blind spots that you can find in Marx as a political theorist. It would seem rather obvious to say that when the Communists tried to organize the atomized masses for the overthrow of their exploiters, the exploiters would not simply sit by and let themselves be overthrown. They would themselves try to get support among these atomized masses in order to ward off the attack. There is, however, no anticipation of this in either Marx or Engels, or even Lenin. They thought of the revolutionary struggle purely in terms of a weakening capitalist structure which eventually toppled of its own weight with only a little push from the revolutionaries. In the dynamic sense that I have portrayed it, Fascism is a response which is surely quite in keeping with the laws of politics. Whenever a political movement starts within any context, there is bound to be a counter movement on the part of those whose interests are affected. What happens in Fascism is that the proletariat is replaced by the nation as the collective reference point in terms of which the deployment of revolutionary violence is justified. Fascism is quite the opposite of Communism, as in it the state receives its positive over-evaluation. This is particularly true in Italian Fascism which harks back directly to Hegel and talks about the state as the real receptacle of the values, interests and beliefs of the community and hence as the vehicle for the effective manipulation of the community and the individuals within it. The views of Hitler and his National Socialists, the German Fascists, are largely the echo of the Italian Fascists who, in these matters, developed notions like "discipline," "hierarchy," and eventually the glorification of war. It is interesting and important to realize that Hitler, by substituting the race for the nation as the focal point for the collective reference, gave himself something that was intrinsically more easily manipulated than had been the older notion of the nation. But like nation, race, too, is fundamentally still an exclusive, instead of an inclusive notion. It is possible to conclude the *Communist Manifesto* by the exclamation: "Proletarians of all the world unite; you have nothing to lose br. your chains"; but one cannot very easily say "Italians of all .ne world unite, you have nothing to lose but your American citizenship." There is no appeal in this so the result is that there is not the world-wide force behind Fascism that had developed behind Communism.

But in either case, the problem of imperialism arises. In the case of the Communists, the imperialism is disguised behind the façade of the dictatorship of the proletariat, but it has become evident in the stresses and conflicts that have rent the Communist bloc. Stalin's was an extreme view, but his basic contention that what is good for the Soviet Union is good for Communism and the world revolution expresses the implicit imperialist thrust which has remained. It is of course more patent in the case of the Fascists and Nazis. Mussolini's oratory about the grandeur that was Rome's and the *imperium Romanum* that must be resurrected are the logical consequence of the Fascist creed. Similarly Hitler's idea of the Greater Europe under Nazi leadership and domination is nothing but the outward thrust of the imperialist implications of his racist notions.

In all three versions of totalitarian thinking there is contained a radical elitism. The notion of an elite predestined to lead and rule is intrinsic in those doctrines.

In a good part of what I have said today there was implied something which you find in the *Communist Manifesto;* namely, that since you obviously could not have all proletarians understand so subtle and complicated a theory of society as is contained in the three volumes of *Das Kapital,* there had to be some kind of a sorting out. This brings us directly to the Marxist idea of the Communists as the class-conscious elite of the proletariat. The Communists are the people who really understand the scientific insight of Karl Marx and therefore are in a position to act in accordance with the historical analysis, or if you prefer, prophecy of Marx.

This notion of an elite is by no means something wholly new; indeed, it has very ancient roots. The doctrine of the elite is a very important part of the political philosophy of Plato and Aristotle. It plays an important role in many religions.

The distinctive feature of Marxist doctrine, however, is that this idea of elitism so widely scattered and held throughout history, is given a very specific content in terms of a scientific understanding of the historic and societal process. This is something that the older elite theories never did. They always thought in terms of ethical notions and in terms of insights into what is good, true and beautiful. In Marxism, as we have seen today, the elitist insight is not into the idea of what is good, true or beautiful but into the process of history. The elite can perceive the dialectic of history, and consequently the necessary future of mankind. Those who possess this "scientific insight" are prepared to provide the leadership in the revolutionary struggle for the realization of Marxist social justice.

READINGS, SUGGESTED AND REQUIRED

Lectures 3 and 4:

REQUIRED READING:

ISAIAH BERLIN, *Karl Marx* (Galaxy).

KARL MARX and FRIEDRICH ENGELS, *Basic Writings on Politics and Philosophy* (Anchor), items I–II, IV–VI, IX, XVII.

SUGGESTIONS FOR FURTHER READING:

HANNAH ARENDT, *Origins of Totalitarianism* (Meridian).

HANNAH ARENDT, "Tradition and the Modern Age," in *Between Past and Future* (Viking).

CRANE BRINTON, *Anatomy of a Revolution* (Smith, Peter).

C. J. FRIEDRICH and Z. K. BRZEZINSKI, *Totalitarian Dictatorship and Autocracy* (Harvard).

V. I. LENIN, *"What is To Be Done?"; The State and Revolution* (International Press).

HERBERT MARCUSE, *Soviet Marxism* (Vintage).

KARL MARX, *Early Writings,* tr. Bottomore (McGraw-Hill).

Readings on Fascism and National Socialism (Swallow).

Revolution, ed. C. J. Friedrich, Nomos VII (Atherton Press).

Social Justice, ed. Richard B. Brandt (Prentice-Hall).

J. L. TALMON, *Origins of Totalitarian Democracy* (Praeger).

ROBERT TUCKER, *Philosophy and Myth in Karl Marx* (Cambridge).

5

Justice and the Function of the
Political Elite

JUSTICE IS ONE of the central topics of all political theory. It is the very heart of Plato's thought. Disturbed by the chaos of his native city Athens he came to conclude that only an elite of philosophers, guardians of truth and justice, could hope to re-establish good government. Thus he became the founder of the elitist theories of politics. But before we examine his ideas proper, we shall have to undertake a general theoretical analysis of the problems of justice and the elite. Both ideas have very ancient roots. Wherever men have reflected upon government, they have done so in terms of justice. How can rulers be made to rule justly is one of the basic questions of politics. The notion that such just rule can only be secured by forming an elite turns up in a number of the great religions. In Christian doctrine it is bound up with the hierarchy and authority of the church, and with the doctrine of predestination. In Confucianism, the good ruler is the wise man learned in the writings of Confucius. In the great religion of India, Hinduism, elitism is involved in the caste system with its pinnacle, the Brahmin. In other words, elitist doctrines are very widespread and somehow linked to man's search for good government.

In Marx's system, this ancient tradition has re-appeared in a new and different form. In the *Communist Manifesto* and other writings, Marx and Engels claim an elitist position for the Communists, not as a party, but as the members of the proletariat with a special understanding of the course of history. Thus they say: "They (the Communists) have over the great mass of the proletariat the advantage of clearly understanding the line of march, the conditions and the ultimate general results of the proletarian movement." Hence it is not moral or philosophical knowledge, but historical and scientific grasp which constitute the elite of the proletariat. Yet even here, the relation is to justice through the belief in social justice we have already discussed. So the question before us is the meaning of the elite and the relation it bears to the realization of justice in a political community. Everybody nowadays talks of elites. This was not always the case. Though it is actually a very old notion it was not always so fashionable a term. Political thought has recurrently been inclined to assert that governing calls for specially qualified men of exceptional capacity, virtue and intelligence. This has been a much more generally accepted and wide-spread idea than the opposing one which became current in America at the beginning of the nineteenth century, namely that everybody was qualified to exercise the functions of government. This idea is traditionally associated with the Jacksonian Revolution, but also sprang up in the American Revolution, when it was ardently expounded by Samuel Adams here in Massachusetts. These men who founded the American Republic or rather helped found it, thought that the task of government did not call for exceptional capacity, virtue and intelligence. There were, however, just as many, if not more, who were of the opinion that it did. Hamilton and quite a few others among the men in Philadelphia certainly shared the elite notion.

When this elitist position is stated in the history of political thought as it is today by a great many people, serious questions are raised. One central question is whether elitism refers to an elite merely in terms of a classification. In other words, does it merely mean that in government and in politics there are a certain number of people who are "good at politics," although they do not operate as a group? And if so, what does "good at politics" mean? Can it be understood in the same way in which other kinds of technical excellence are seen and evaluated? Can rulers be equated with doctors, cooks and other sorts of technicians? Men like Plato thought they could, and in our time Vilfredo Pareto has made himself the exponent of this idea. It is argued that it is possible to classify any kind of artisans and performers according to the quality of their performance, and then to arrange them in such a way that the best are in a small class by themselves; these you then call the elite. The elite of the medical profession would be best at doctoring and the elite of the profession of the cooks would be the ones best at cooking, and so forth and so on. For every professional activity you can identify a small number of people who are doing the job best; these would be the elite. This, however, would merely be an objective classification of individuals according to their quality, because there is no necessary connection between them. These best ones would not necessarily be grouped together as friends, nor would they even necessarily cooperate. In fact they may be the very ones in the fiercest competition with each other just because they are the best.

Now is there really an analogy to this when we speak of best in governing? Abstractly speaking there undoubtedly is. We can abstractly admit that scattered through the land there are a small number of people who are best at government. In reality, however, it is another question entirely when it comes to identifying them, to ascertaining who they are. When you talk about the doctor, the cook, the shoemaker, or other kinds of concrete crafts, identifying the best practitioner is rather simple. People wear shoes and will say "this is a good shoe," or "this is not a good shoe." People eat dinners and they can say "well, this is a wonderful meal," or "this meal tastes bad." In such cases where one evaluates the performance of a concrete craft one can thus identify the best performers by merely consulting the users. With government, however, the situation is not so easy. The value to be realized in connection with government is not one which is itself easily identified. In cooking, it is the meal; in doctoring, it is health and in various other professions it is always some definite value which is to be realized. When that particular value is realized in a superior way it can be said that this man is part of the elite of his profession who realize their craft in a superior way. With government, however, the difficulty arises that people who are its consumers disagree as to what is to be done. Unlike the users and consumers of shoes and meals and various other things, they are not inclined to be in agreement. Indeed, quite the contrary, the tendency is to be more or less in disagreement. Even in a country as relatively homogeneous as the United States it is quite obvious that people disagree on the tasks of government. You need only think of the development in Selma. A rather large group of people who constitute the vital electorate in Alabama still think the governor who ordered the police to maltreat the marchers was a great governor faithfully executing his duty. The people who are marching and a great many others in this land think he is a terrible governor and that he is quite wrong. This kind of disagreement is very characteristic of the task of government. In government, the goals are themselves continually in dispute and consequently if one asks: who is the best governor, the answer is moot, and hence it remains quite uncertain as to who the elite is.

Leaving the problem of a mere classification of an elite aside we must now turn to the political factors presumably present in an elitist situation. Is it not really implicit in the idea of a political or governing elite that it possess some cohesion, some sense and capacity of acting jointly as a group to realize values it shares? When we speak of a party, we usually think in terms of such a cohesive group. When people refer to a political or governing elite I think they do imply some organized group which hangs together, thinks alike and is able to act jointly. In the common understanding elite conjures up the image of some *calculated group conspiracy* to hold and utilize political power.

An American author, the late C. Wright Mills, has stirred up a great deal of discussion in the United States by depicting American politics in terms of this notion of a cohesive elite. In his book *The Power Elite* written some ten years ago, he asserted that there had arisen in the United States a group which he called the "power elite." In his opinion this elite was running the country, contrary to America's alleged democratic theory of pluralistic participation in the determination of public policy. Let me quote a key sentence from this book. "The political directorate, the corporate rich and the higher military have come together as the power elite." It is important to note that he believes them consciously and purposefully to have formed this cohesive group; he also thinks that "the expanded and centralized hierarchies which they head have encroached upon the old balances and have now relegated them to the middle levels of power." In short, it is asserted that we now have in the United States a power elite which runs the country. This view has by no means been universally acclaimed. Quite on the contrary, it has been almost universally criticized. It has been questioned most cogently by a political scientist, Robert Dahl, who found through an exhaustive study that in New Haven no such elite could be located. He found that there does not exist *one* group which decides all important questions, but rather that—quite in keeping with the theory of pluralistic democracy—different groups are formed for particular decisions and fields of policy, often forming spontaneously in response to challenges in particular problem areas. Many political and other social scientists feel that the same constellations would be found to exist in other American cities, and indeed on the level of state and national government. In any case, considerable doubt persists as to the actual operative reality of any kind of power elite in the United States. I am not going to pursue this argument any further because we are here concerned with the general problem of a political elite rather than the concrete question as to the existence at the present time of such an elite in the United States. I mentioned the work of these two men to show you that this is really a very pressing issue in the United States which cannot be handled without being clear in one's own mind as to what such an elite would be.

Mills' argument raises, however, another important theoretical issue. Let us, for the sake of the argument, assume that he were correct in his insistence that a certain small number of corporate magnates, key bureaucrats and high military run the United States. But do these people consider themselves a cohesive group ruling America, and do they share some purposes or goals which they as a group seek to realize? Mills failed to provide any evidence in support of such a premise and many doubt that it could be furnished. Until it is, Mills' arguments amount essentially to the proposition that one can group those on top of various piles as being "in charge"—a fairly circular argument.

There is no doubt that elites have existed in the past. It has always been generally recognized, however, that it is very difficult to locate them in a functioning democracy. In the past elites have been typically based on three things: on blood descent, on riches, or on military prowess. The elite in aristocratic England of the eighteenth century was an elite based primarily on blood descent and riches. The same thing was true in Venice. In some countries such as eighteenth-century Prussia, the elite was based on blood descent and military prowess. It is possible to compare and analyze cases of elite dominance in an attempt comparatively to derive an over-all theory of a political governing elite. The result of such an inquiry would be in my opinion the following conclusion: an elite is a group of people who are distinguished by an exceptional performance in politics, who effectively monopolize the rule of a particular community in their hands and who possess a sense of group cohesion and a corresponding *ésprit de corps* as the French call it, usually expressed in cooptation. The term "cooptation" in this context means that the elite itself decides whom to take into the charmed circle. This may be done in an aristocratic way by giving particular persons titles of nobility, a practice still used in England. The elitist legacy is still powerful even with a Labour government. The socialists still feel it essential and important to put the stamp of approval on deserving participants in the fight for power by giving them a title of nobility. It has, however, become increasingly estranged from its original purpose of providing reinforcements for the political elite. The recent knightings of singers, dancers and acrobats, have produced sharp protests on the part of people who sense the devaluation of what was once an important instrument in the hands of a political elite or ruling class. (It is important, in this connection, to realize that a ruling class may be not a class which rules but the class from which the rulers are taken.) Cooptation has always been as important to elites and aristocracies as election has been to democracies. It is still a very characteristic aspect of English political life. If you want to summarize this brief and theoretical discussion you could say that a political and governing elite excels in the ability to secure power and to rule. From that position of eminence it determines which values shall prevail in a particular community, which values shall be expressed in public policy, and which values shall be realized in governmental operations.

In the United States, we have, I believe, only one such elite, with limited, but nonetheless very crucial, functions. This is the elite of the law. The elite of the law seems inherent in our system. It was recognized as such in the nineteenth century by that astute observer of American institutions, Alexis de Tocqueville. The elite of the law is often not included in descriptions of the power elite. This omission may reflect the problem of the orientation of this elite. Is it oriented towards power or towards justice? In any case the elite of the law-men is in-built in America because the community rests on a Constitution which is a basic law. The interpretation of that Constitution is a crucial element in the functioning of American society and it can only be undertaken by people who understand the law. The layman can read the Constitution, but that does not mean that he can say what it means. He can have his notions about it, but they are as like as not quite wrong. The layman must be told by the legal fraternity why he is wrong in his reading of the law and what is the right way of putting it. This elite of the law defends its primacy against the attempts of certain other groups in the American community to arrogate to themselves specific governing elite functions. These competing groups may install themselves in certain corners of the land and try to develop an elitist formation. The elite of the law comes along, however, and smashes them. When it does this there is usually a big howl heard in the land. But since the constitutional system is still in operation the howl subsides and that particular would-be elite in the corner goes out of existence. We have experienced this process only recently. Part of the drama of this decade in which you are spending your time in college reflects this competition in the Supreme Court decisions on segregation and reapportionment. Here are two areas in which the law elite is proceeding against groups which have arrogated to themselves extra-constitutional powers; they have, in other words, appointed themselves as local elites. Now they are being smoked out and destroyed by the law elite.

This raises a question which is, in my opinion, the crucial problem in connection with elite formation. I refer to the question of justice. We have so far spoken only of law. There looms, however, the important question which permeates all these discussions at the present time, namely, whether law is identical with justice. Can one say that whatever is legal is just? Must one be more cautious and say no, a law may be but is not necessarily just? The further question then arises: who determines the problems which present themselves when there is a conflict between law and justice? There is at least one conventional answer to this last question which says that whenever there is a conflict between law and justice it is for the legislature to settle the problem of law and justice by making the law more just by bringing it into accord with ideas of justice. In this country, of course, we have the Constitution and the legislature cannot by itself change the Constitution. One might then say that the power to amend the Constitution accommodates law to what is just. It is not an easy thing, however, to change the Constitution. Often the change of the Constitution has been slow in coming while in the meantime the law was being re-interpreted and thus to some extent adjusted.

The emphasis in the common law tradition and in the American constitutional adoption of that tradition is that in this interval before the law is adjusted by those in charge of changing the law, whether it be the ordinary law or the law of the Constitution, the power of the judge applies. It is the task of the judge, whom we call the "justice," to try to the best of his ability to aid in the realization of justice by re-interpreting the law.

There is involved here a great question which has agitated political and juristic thought for centuries; that is the question of whether laws which are not just are laws. Some very great thinkers have answered this question in the negative. Cicero, for example, asserts very explicitly that a law which is not just is not truly a law. The same position is taken by St. Thomas Aquinas. In his famous *Summa* on theology he wrote that a law which was not just could not be said to possess truly the quality of a law. This I think is going too far. These thinkers were right in pointing out that there is a difference between a law which is just and a law which is not just. But I personally think that we get at this difference more satisfactorily by saying that the latter law is an inferior kind of law or an imperfect law, a law that requires alteration and change. You might express this in another way by saying that it is a law which lacks authority. I will come back to this problem of authority. But I think you will recognize that it is possible to say that an unjust law has less authority. For example, when Adolf Hitler made the laws of racial persecution which some Germans found very unsatisfactory and not in keeping with their tradition, those laws had less authority than other laws which also prevailed and which were also applied. One gets into a hopeless mess in terms of a concrete political and legal order if, as Cicero and Aquinas, one insists that a law which is not just is not a law. There is no doubt that laws are continually enforced about whose justice there is considerable controversy.

There is always of course the additional problem as to who decides whether a law is just. Who determines whether a law is just? I might mention here without trying to get into the depths of this argument that the problem which I have just presented to you is related to another very extended and still very active issue in law and politics, and that is whether law is a command or whether it is a rule of reason, whether it is an act of will or whether it is an act of reason. You might say that this is a rather theoretical question, and indeed it is; but it is a question with the most extraordinary practical ramifications. If it is a rule of reason, such was for example the view of Thomas Aquinas, you have much more and much better grounds for distinguishing between laws which are just and laws which are not, because the laws which are not just are the laws which are not in accord with reason. If you say they are not in accord with reason you have some basis for a discussion of their degree of justness. It is then a question of disputing about the reasonableness of the law. On the other hand if you say that the law is an act of will, the only question which you have to ascertain is who is the one whose will decides. In the great days of the emergence of the modern state a writer like Bodin alleged that it was necessary to have one sovereign because law was in essence a decision of the will, and only one will could decide what the law would be. The greatest in this school of believers that law is an act of will was Thomas Hobbes who made this one of the central points of his very radical political theory. We will come back to Hobbes later; here I merely want to call your attention to the fact that the problem of whether law is a command or a rule of reason is behind this question of the justice or the injustice of the law.

We must now follow out the other side of the issue, namely what is justice. You remember that when we talked about social justice we found that it was taken to be more or less a general principle of equal treatment for every member of the community; this includes of course equality before the law. There are other and in some ways profounder issues connected with the problem of such treatment. They spring from the justice aspect of such treatment rather than the social aspect. If one asks what really is the characteristic feature of justice, one finds that the problem can be discussed in two different ways. You can discuss this question in the way Plato primarily did, namely in terms of the justice of a man and the analogous justice of the political order. Or you can discuss it in terms of the justice of an act, such as a law, or any other kind of act, governmental or otherwise. I would prefer to deal today with the political side of justice, that is to say with justice in relation to the political act and situation. An action and hence also a rule, a judgment, a decision or a law may be said to be just when it involves the comparative evaluation of the persons affected by the act, and when that comparison shows that the act accords with the values and beliefs of the community. A comparative evaluation of the persons means that these persons are not treated as basically alike, but rather as basically different. One must evaluate people in order to make sure that an act is just. We do not usually think an act just when everyone is treated like everyone else. We want the criminal, for example, to be treated differently from the honest man; we want a child to be treated differently from a grown man; and we want a person in an official position to be treated differently from a private person, and so forth and so on. All laws are shot through with differentiation and consequently with what I call comparative evaluation of the persons involved in the situation. This evaluation must also accord with the values and beliefs of the community. The values and beliefs of the community determine the equality of judgments. Aristotle first developed this in terms of his contrast between arithmetic and geometric justice. Geometric justice would differentiate people by saying that no one should be treated on the basis of simple arithmetic, one to one equality, but on the basis of an equality which considered the proportionate value of the particular person involved.

A very serious and difficult question arises in this connection. If we say that the justice of an action is actually determined by the extent to which it succeeds in differentiating between persons in accordance with the values and beliefs of the community, are we not confronted with the problem of impartiality? Justice has always been thought of in terms of impartiality but on close inspection it is clear that a just action is not an impartial action. We allow women and children to leave a sinking boat first rather than the fellow who is first at the lifeboat because we differentiate between women, children and men. We are thus not being impartial towards women and children. As one looks at societies' actions he sees that in order to be just, one needs to be partial to him who is entitled to more than someone else. What then remains of this problem of impartiality that is so frequently stated and with, I think, a sense behind it that is right? What remains is that the action must not be *arbitrary*. Our partiality must be in accordance with the values and the beliefs of the community. It must be consistent; it must be continually the same kind of partiality towards the same kind of person in the same kind of situation. On the other hand, impartiality also implies another important distinction and that is the recognition that we must avoid asking the impossible of people. The arbitrary and the impossible we must avoid. There is a famous old Latin legal principle, *ultra posse nemo obligatur,* beyond that which he can do, nobody is obliged to act.

I recommend this dictum to you particularly because in our time there has been a very despicable tendency on the part of some people to moralize about people in other political contexts and demand that they do things which in the nature of things they cannot do. For example, we tend continually to ask of people subject to totalitarian autocracy that they act as if they were in our position and thus to act like free citizens in a pluralistic democracy. But people who are subject to totalitarian dictatorships are in no position to act that way. When we expect them to act that way—and it does not matter whether they are Russians, Poles, Chinese or Germans—we are hypocrites and hypocrisy is one of the violations of the standards of justice in terms of impartiality.

The problem of justice also immediately involves the problem of injustice. Injustice is related to what today we call "disvalues" and "disbeliefs." When looked at psychologically, it is clear that people react more violently to claims of injustice than they do to those of justice. Curiously enough, the emotional reaction to justice is weaker than that to injustice. When observing an unjust act the beholder is seized with anxiety. He feels a tremor, so to speak, in his world of values. Hence he tends to view every unjust act as an attack upon the political order of the society in which he lives. By questioning or putting into jeopardy the values and beliefs of the community, injustice affects many people. The non-realization of justice, however, does not affect anyone who does not happen to be involved in that particular situation. Basically, of course, this is not a dichotomy, but it merely suggests that we continually are confronted in the problem of justice by the "more" or "less." You might put it this way: the conflict situation in which this problem of justice or injustice arises is one demanding a comparative judgment of whether the particular action proposed is *more* or *less* just. Generally speaking we can say that the kinds of things people want to do are neither wholly unjust nor wholly just, but always somewhere in between.

This leads me to the concluding reflection that I want to lay before you today and that is the relation of justice to reason and reasoning. It is here that we see the crucial interaction of ideas on justice and elitism. When we speak of a judge as just we mean, among other things, that he can give us a good reason if we question his decision. In the United States this has become so profound a conviction on the part of the community that we actually invite our judges to offer their opinions in printed form. We even encourage the dissenting judge to give his counter-opinion on why he does not agree with his colleagues. This is done so that the legal community, and beyond it anyone who is interested, lawmen and laymen, can examine these reasons and try to reach a decision about the justice of the act in terms of the reasons given for it. This implies a commitment in a very interesting and curious way to truth which is just as relevant politically as the commitment to justice. I will give you a very simple illustration to make this point. Suppose you heard that a particular decision of a judge and jury had been based on inadequate evidence, that the things considered in arriving at the decision were not the whole truth but only part of the truth, and that if you took the other part into consideration you would possibly arrive at a different decision. No doubt you immediately would agree that the just thing would be to review the decision and to consider the whole case once again in light of the new evidence. This is indeed recognized in our legal order where if new evidence turns up a re-trial can be ordered. Many times, of course, there is a vigorous and particularly sharp argument about whether a particular body of evidence does constitute "new" evidence or not. Elaborate rules have been developed about that. This means that we can never separate the problem of how just a particular act is from the question about how close to truth the reasons are upon which the particular just act is based. That, of course, means it is always an open question because to those of us who are committed to the ways of modern science truth is an open question. What might be true is never a settled question.

At this point we are getting to the great and I think fundamental issue we confront with Plato and all the elitists down through the ages. Plato based his elitist argument on his conviction in absolute truth. The absolute truth could be found by a certain elite group and when it had been found it had to be made the basis of all political actions under this group's direction. There is absolutely no question that if the premise is correct, the conclusion follows. If there is such a thing as absolute truth and if there is a demonstrable way of finding the absolute truth, then there is no question that those who have found it ought to be put in charge as a governing elite to decide what is justice as well as what particular actions are just. There has been a very serious question about this Platonic elitism for a very long time. In our democratic society there has been a general inclination to think that justice is controversial and not absolute and certain. It can only be argued over and settled ad hoc for the particular issue at the particular time and must be reconsidered at the next issue and in the next situation. With no absolute truth there is no need for an elite group; the pretended ability to know such a truth is revealed as an ideological façade for a power drive. In our time, these particular anti-elitist attitudes which arose in the West in connection with the development of democratic societies have been reinforced by the conflict of cultures. It is reinforced on the one hand by our everyday experience of there being radical differences of opinion among Indians, Chinese, Americans and Russians as to what is truth and what is just and the experience of clashes between these views whenever international relations are involved. This cultural relativity or equality is one of the reasons why the colonial situation is untenable in the twentieth century. In the twentieth century the old generally-held belief in some kind of absolute justice to which only some small group of white men had access has completely disintegrated.

I would like to conclude today by citing a very impressive literary example which illustrates in some way what I have been trying to say in the second half of this lecture. It is from a novel, *Man in a Mirror,* published three years ago by a Welshman, Llewelyn. This story is set in East Africa and deals with a native who is brought before a court because he has killed a man who had himself killed a cow. In terms of our own value judgments and beliefs there is no question that somebody who kills a man simply because the man had killed a cow must be punished for murder. The English lawyer who decided to defend this native was correspondingly handicapped by culturally different views. He tried his best to argue for his client within the English system of law, but of course he lost his case and the native was condemned. The passage which interests me finds the Englishman asking an African friend whether he did not think he had done a fine job in presenting the case. The African friend Niterenka replied that he thought he had done as well as he knew how. "But you might have presented the case with more knowledge of what it is a 'masai' feels. Our language is very different. Our life is also very different. A translation into English words is not enough. Our traditions, our feelings also must be translated. Your law is not our law, and to us cattle are just as important as people. That is an absolute fact." Truth then is different, and so is justice for different people at different times. Particular elites may be able to contribute their share to the crystallizing of opinion as to what they are, but only the people at large can, so democratic theory holds, settle the differences by enunciating what the community believes and values.

6

Plato's Idea of Justice and the Political Elite

W HEN ONE SAYS: Plato, he also says: Socrates. For no one has ever succeeded in really settling the issue as to whether it is Socrates or Plato who speaks to us from the great Platonic Dialogues. One very interesting thing about Plato is that although people have written about him for these several thousand years as if he spoke for himself through the Socrates of his Dialogues, he himself wrote down for us in his Second Letter the following very striking and puzzling sentence as an answer to what Dionysius, the tyrant of Syracuse, had written about him: "I have never written anything about it, nor does there exist any writing of Plato about it, nor will there be. And what one now calls that, that is by Socrates." Plato in this Second Letter makes it very clear that he considered his own views to be a kind of unwritten secret doctrine, something that he would not publicize, something that he would discuss only in the Academy which he founded. About the teaching there we know something from Aristotle and others who were students in the Academy.

There is little doubt that Plato was a very great man and a greater figure in the history of political thought than even Karl Marx. At the same time I think we need to temper our admiration of this great philosopher and bear in mind an ancient saying about him which in light of his own thinking he himself could hardly question. *Magnus amicus Plato maior amica veritas,* a great friend is Plato, but a greater friend is the truth. And where should we more readily remember this than at Harvard! I mention this partly because there are some very striking conflicts between Plato's ideas and American ideals. No one has put this more dramatically than Jefferson, who somewhere described Plato's ideas as "nonsense." He wrote, "In truth Plato is one of the greatest of genuine Sophists, and it is regrettable that there occurred an adoption and incorporation of his whimsies into the body of an artificial Christianity. His foggy mind is always presenting the semblances of objects. The Christian priesthood finding the doctrines of Christ levelled to every man's understanding and too plain to need explanation saw in the mysticism of Plato materials from which they could build up an artificial system which might from its indistinctness admit of everlasting controversy and give employment to their order and introduce it to profit, power and preeminence." This condemnation of Plato for his influence on Christian thought is a very striking statement and I think in many ways worth pondering. I add to Jefferson's an evaluation of Plato by Brandeis, one of the great Justices of the Supreme Court. "His must be recognized to be the most theoretical nonsensical plan that human ingenuity ever invented." You see these two great Americans did not mince words in expressing themselves negatively about Plato's political thought.

We know relatively little about Plato's life. He was the scion of a great aristocratic family of Athens. After some unsuccessful dabbling in practical politics he retired and became a teacher of wisdom in that Academy which he founded and which has always been looked upon as the origin and beginning of our university system, so striking a feature of Western civilization.

You are being asked in this course to read what is perhaps his greatest work, commonly called *The Republic* or the State. The central theme of this work is the one which occupies us here today, namely, justice. Indeed, in some of the old manuscripts the title of the work is *About Justice* rather than *About the State*. Two questions are central to his discussion of justice: (1) What is justice? (2) How can it be achieved? When he asks what is justice, he is concerned with its particular embodiment in the just man and the just city. This is, you will remember, the problem which I put aside last time when I talked about justice and politics. In addition to these basic questions about the just man and the just city, Plato also asks at the very outset of the work: "Why should a man be just?" This question and its possible answers had agitated thoughtful people in Greece and in the "Greater Greece," which was Sicily, for much of the preceding century. The sophist movement was itself a response to the problem of why a man should be just. Would it not be sufficient, the sophist asked, for a man merely to appear just rather than to be just? It is not difficult to understand why such a concern was at the heart of the teaching of the sophists. The word sophist originally meant just "teacher." They were the teachers who thrived in the great Sicilian and Greek cities; and their major task was to show a man how he could succeed in public life, how he could succeed in politics. If such success is the primary objective it is impossible to avoid the problem of whether you succeed by being just or whether you succeed by being unjust, in other words, whether you succeed by appearing just while actually not being just.

One can, in a sense, easily answer this question, "what is just?" in strictly political terms, the way I did in Lecture V when I said that to be just is to act in accordance with the values and beliefs of the community. In such a case, then, the just man is the man who acts justly, who takes just actions; that is to say, in accordance with what the community to which he belongs believes. In this simple approach there arises, however, precisely the problem that occupied Plato and that occupied his contemporaries. What if there is a confusion about values and beliefs; what if there is a general alienation, as we nowadays would say, of the ancient faith upon which the values and beliefs had once rested? When the community's values and beliefs are uncertain you cannot say that the just man is he who acts in accordance with these values and beliefs, because this reference point is precisely the one that is in dispute. The Greeks had a word to describe this situation which has recently come into use in our Western languages, *anomie*. It is derived from *nomos*. Nomos means ancient custom based on ancient conviction; and anomie, therefore, implies that state in which there is no longer any such nomos, any such ancient custom or ancient conviction as to what is right. Perhaps one of the reasons why this whole discussion of justice and community standards is now of such great and, I would almost say, of such absorbing concern to us in the twentieth century, is that we feel that we live in just such a state of anomie, a state in which values and beliefs have become uncertain and a matter of dispute. The problem of what is the right way to live has once again, as in Athens in the fifth century, become a matter of controversy.

Plato's answer to those who seek the nature of justice is an answer which does not appeal to a great many Americans. But it does appeal to some of the people who now present themselves under the general label of conservatives or neo-conservatives. Generally, however, unlike Plato, such conservatives are inclined to go back to what they consider the ancient verities. They are inclined to say that in order to be able to answer the question as to what is right conduct, we must try to revive the ancient faith. Plato, however, was much more radical than these conservatives and neo-conservatives, indeed more radical than the conservatives of his own day. He realized that you cannot revive a faith that is gone merely on the basis of its political desirability. You cannot increase piety and belief in God merely because it is a helpful thing to believe in God. This is not the way to create a belief in God. Plato, the profound and radical philosopher, therefore said "Belief must rest on ratiocination. Knowledge must take the place of opinion."

The starting point of Plato's quest for justice is, in a sense, rather simple. The just man can be discovered by looking for the just city, which is the just man writ large. If we can work out what is the just city, then by analogous reasoning we will be able to say what is the just man. With this purpose Socrates and his interlocutors in *The Republic* venture forth into a discussion of the just city. Lest you be perplexed by the way in which the dialogue begins, remember that it was not uncommon in Greece for people to set out and found a new city. Often, if the Greek polis, a small and confined town, became overcrowded, a certain group of people got together, manned a boat and set forth on the blue Mediterranean to found a new city. In other words, what Socrates and his friends talk about at the start of *The Republic* was related to a common experience in the real world of many Greeks. Americans should feel somewhat congenial to this approach because, after all, their country as contrasted to old Europe is one actually founded by just such people who got on a boat and set out to found a new commonwealth. In any case, it is with such a new city that Plato begins his search for justice.

Plato proceeds to a rather elaborate argument illustrating how a just city should be organized. But the central principle is a rather simple one. In order that a city be just, its rulers must be just. But how can one be sure that rulers will be just? The answer given by Plato has echoed down through the ages. Rulers must be seekers after wisdom. This is the famous passage found in *The Republic,* p. 473, D: "Unless the lovers of wisdom become rulers in cities, or those who are now called kings or rulers become genuine and adequate lovers of wisdom, and political power and wisdom are brought together, and unless the numerous natures who at present pursue either politics or philosophy the one to the exclusion of the other, are forcibly debarred from this behavior, there will be no respite from evil, not for cities nor for humanity. . . ." In many translations, this statement is made to read: "philosophers" rather than "lovers of wisdom." But this distorts Plato's meaning, especially if one thinks of a "philosopher" as a professor of philosophy, political or other. The lover or seeker after wisdom is closer to a Confucian or Buddhist sage than to the logician and systematizer.

Of course, such rational elitism does not exhaust Plato's program for a just city. It has a number of interesting corollaries. For one, there is equality of men and women, at least in the guardian class. It is often spoken of as a communism of wives, but this way of putting the matter is misleading; for men and women are treated quite alike, and they are intended to eat and live together and have no private life of their own. Besides this guardian class, two other classes are recognized by Plato-Socrates, namely warriors and the artisans. The argument about these classes so closely resembles the ideas associated with the Indian caste system that it has at times been surmised that Socrates and Plato must have come into contact with travelers from India in one of the trading cities of Ionia (Asia Minor), but it is not necessary to explain the matter in this way. The notion flows quite naturally and logically from Plato's belief that everyone should be content to do the task for which he is suited, and that justice means balance and harmony. Indeed, this is the key to the problem of justice in the city as in the soul. In some ways, this image of a city with a static class structure is probably an idealized version of what had at an earlier time been the actual organization of a typical Greek *polis*. But instead of the religious faith of the forefathers, it is now founded upon the philosophical insight of the wise guardians who rule the city rationally.

No wonder that Jefferson thought little of Plato and his "foggy mind" full of "sophisms and futilities." Such thoughts are about as far removed from the dynamic politics of America as one can be. The Marxist elitism has some features of it. But instead of the wise guardians, the class-conscious elite of the proletariat who understand the laws of history and dialectical materialism are the predestined leaders. By contrast, it is Plato's message that unless lovers of wisdom become rulers, there cannot be a just city. In order to become fit for this task of ruling, Plato goes on, the rulers must undergo the ordeal of discovering the true good. The great traditional Greek formula, you know, was *kalos k'agathos,* "the beautiful and the good." In *The Republic* Plato was concerned with the ethical part, the "agathos." The "kalos," which for Plato was equally significant, was treated in another dialogue called *The Symposium* or *The Banquet.* I have always regretted that we cannot also assign *The Symposium* in this course, because in my view it is only by taking these two dialogues together that you have the complete Plato on politics. If you take only *The Republic* with its emphasis on the "good" and the "just," Plato has too moralistic a flavor which must be complemented by the aesthetic flavor of *The Symposium,* with its emphasis on the beautiful. It is useful to look at *The Symposium* for one other important reason. This dialogue contains Plato's discussion of love, a subject not usually germane to political theory. But it is very much to our purposes here because in Plato's view the good ruler is the *lover* of wisdom. In *The Symposium* Plato relates this love of wisdom to other manifestations of love. A few crucial quotations may give the flavor of this dialogue which acts as a kind of balance for what you will be reading in *The Republic.*

The Symposium, to explain their setting, tells of a banquet in a house of a wealthy Athenian. The participants in the banquet decide to see who can praise love most effectively. After several brilliant speeches, Socrates is asked to have his say. In his speech of praise Socrates describes an experience he had in his youth when he encountered a sage woman, the Diotima from whom he learned the crucial insights on love and learning upon which all his life has been built. It is from Diotima's instructions and Socrates' fine conclusion that I want to cite "By far the most important kind of wisdom is that which governs the ordering of society and that which goes by the name of justice and moderation." Such pronouncements clearly indicate the fundamental unity of the Platonic message to be found in *The Republic* and *The Symposium.* Socrates, then, describes Diotima's instructions on how one received such wisdom. "In his youth such a person who is a seeker after wisdom would go about in search of the loveliness on which he may beget. Hence his procreant nature is attracted by a comely body rather than an ill-favored one. If he also happens on a soul which is at once beautiful, generous and gentle, he is charmed to find so welcome an alliance. The beauties of the body are, however, as nothing to the beauties of the soul." Socrates then tells that from this he developed an interest in political institutions and in the sciences. "And then," she says, "there bursts upon the wondrous vision of the soul that beauty which he has toiled for so long. This vision will not be of the face or hands, nor of anything that is of flesh. It will be neither words nor knowledge, nor of something that exists in something else, but subsisting of and by itself in an eternal one-ness while every lovely thing partakes of it. This, my dear Socrates, is the only way one must approach or be led towards the sanctuary of love. Starting from individual beauties, the quest for the universal beauty must find him ever mounting the heavenly ladder, stepping from rung to rung. That is from one to two and from two to every lovely body, from bodily beauty to the beauty of institutions, from institutions to learning, from learning in general to the special knowledge that pertains to nothing but beauty itself, until at last he comes to know what beauty is." "Love will help our mortal nature more than all the world." This is the teaching of Diotima. And Socrates adds: "That is why I say that every one of us should worship the God of Love and why I cultivate all the elements of love myself."

This concept of love found in *The Symposium* is necessary in order to appreciate the "philo" part of philosopher, the man who must rule. The first part of this word, the "lover" of wisdom means, for Plato and Socrates, somebody who starts with physical love and ascends gradually to the final love of ultimate wisdom which is the wisdom that comprehends the ideas of beauty and of goodness. This ascension is a long and arduous ordeal, requiring a tremendous intellectual effort. In order to convey something of this effort, Plato tells the famous myth of the Cave in the middle of his dialogue on *The Republic*. I cannot take the time here to tell you this tale in its fullness. What is important to note, from our point of view, is the message of the myth: that men cannot become just unless they perceive the idea of justice. Men cannot perceive the idea of justice unless they detach themselves completely from their earthly concerns and behold the fountainhead of all ideas, the idea of the Good. The idea of the Good is portrayed in Plato's myth as a radiant and brilliant sunlike entity which blinds those who emerge from the Cave. It can be seen only by what it lights up, namely, these other ideas of Justice and Beauty and so on. Those few men who have emerged from the cave, and this is very crucial for Plato, may not, however, remain in contemplation of this eternal verity, the idea of the Good and the other ideas of the Beautiful, the Just, etc. These lovers of wisdom, partakers of absolute truth, must return to the Cave. If they do not return to the Cave it would be clear that they had not really grasped the idea of the Just or the idea of the Good. The return to the cave is symbolic of man's political commitment to realize the good in the polis, to become an actor in accordance with the idea of the good, to shape the earthly city.

At this point I must say a few words about Platonic philosophy and the notion of the Idea. I realize this is no more than a hint, for in order to grasp this fully one would have to spend many hours rather than a few minutes. But I'm doing it here to sort of intrigue you, arouse your interest, and hopefully to incite you to further inquiries. The difficulty arises in part because when Plato uses the word "idea," or frequently the word "idos," he does not mean what we ordinarily mean when we speak of the word "idea." He does not think of something that is primarily a prescription for action but something that is much more nearly aesthetic, something that is grasped by beholding it much the way one perceives a beautiful statue. Perhaps a brief excursion into cultural history will help illustrate my point and make it easier to understand Plato's thought. I do not know whether or not you have ever been struck by the difference between the great achievements of Greek art and the great achievements of Western art. If you have you will probably note that we think that the great achievements, of Rembrandt or Leonardo or of other painters or sculptors are due to their ability to portray the individual and the particular. The subject is not necessarily perfect nor beautiful except in a spiritual sense, like the old woman that Rembrandt painted and which goes under the name of his mother. Art historians do not think it was his mother, but that does not matter. The significant thing is that here Rembrandt has created an individual portrait. If you look, however, at the great works of Greek art like the Venus of Milo, or the Zeus of Praxiteles you will see that they are totally devoid of individuality. They are in the most striking sense abstracted from particularity to arrive at that which is universal. What all Greek artists struggled for was to find the expression universally acceptable as the quintessence of beauty. This same principle is true in architecture. Detractors of Greek art often say that Greek temples are boring, that if you have seen one, you have seen them all. In one sense this is very true. If you go to Greece you will indeed see that if you have seen one, you have seen them all because they are all alike. They are all similar in being efforts to achieve the ultimate, the quintessentially beautiful. Consequently they do not seek to be individual creations, expressing the style of an individual or an age. They are consciously made to be like the others but only better. This sense of an unalterable perfection existing externally to which the Greek artist aspired also operated in the Platonic theory of ideas. Above all particular and individual examples of good and justice there existed the absolute reality and perfection of justice and goodness.

When the question is raised whether the Platonic city is realizable or not, it is necessary to point out that it would be inconceivable that a Greek describe an ideal statue or temple or city that was not realizable. To do so would be absolutely without purpose. It must be realizable if it is to be worthwhile. In addition one should point out the statements from Plato himself. They are quite specific and have to be overlooked if you want to assert that Plato's city was not realizable, that it was a Utopia in the Western sense. In *The Republic,* right after the statement about the philosophers as rulers, there is a passage which states "nor will this constitution which we have just described in our argument come to that realization which is possible." Note the key phrase, "which is possible." A little later on page 499 he makes the reality of his just city even more explicit. "To suppose that either or both of these alternatives is impossible, I maintain to be quite unreasonable. The constitution we have described has arisen, exists and will arise when the muse of philosophy becomes mistress of a city. That she should do so is not impossible. Nor are the things we have described impossible." It would seem to me that Plato could not be more explicit. You would have to say that he did not know what he was talking about if you want to assert that Plato considered his city unrealizable. In his view it was of the essence that it should be realizable. In a sense what he sets forth is the idea of a city in the sense of a realizable essentiality of what a city should be like. That is why it can be a measuring rod. At other places in the book you will see that every city partakes of this idea. Just as every beautiful body and every beautiful ideal partakes of the idea of Beauty, so every city partakes to some extent, be it ever so imperfectly, in this idea of the perfect city which it seeks to realize.

Let us turn to the political implications of these ideas. You know of course that the people who had successfully gone through the arduous ordeal of perceiving the idea of the good and the idea of the just were the elite and fit to become the Guardians. They were fit to be the political leadership of the polis. In a sense what Plato really means is that there are in a city these *"Men of gold,"* who seek wisdom and try to ascertain what is just. They are men of the highest intellect. Obviously not many could undergo this training, not many would make this effort. What Plato has done is to substitute a rational elite of learning for a traditional elite of family and wealth. The traditional Greek polis had its political elite, its guardians. If you read Homer, if you read Theognis or Pindar, the rule of the aristocracy is celebrated. But they were the aristocracy because of inheritance, because of what their ancestors had done. The argument that Plato sets forth is that these are not good foundations for the political ruling class. The foundation must be rational achievement, an achievement of the mind.

In spite of Plato's brave and courageous assertions about the realizability of the perfect city in which the muse of justice reigns, there is found in *The Republic* an undercurrent of despair. Toward the end of the Book, in the Ninth Book, that mood of despair expresses itself in a famous pair of sentences which I would like to cite preliminary to making a brief comment. Plato writes: "In

heaven there is laid up" (and I will give you a conventional translation) "an idea of the polis which he who desires may contem-
plate and seeing it," now the classical translation says: "may set
his home in order." Another translator (Lindsay), however, says
"found a city in himself." But whether such a city exists here on
earth or whether it will exist in fact is no matter. For the wise man
will live after the manner of that *polis* which he has set up in himself and has nothing to do with any other." In other words there
is here a retreat from participation in the concrete life of the city
into an ivory tower of a man who is satisfied with a city within
himself as Lindsay states. Actually both translators are making a
kind of gloss. What Plato says is *heautón katoikídzein* which
means to settle himself, to colonize himself and what he means is
that *if* a man cannot found the just city outside himself *then* he
can found it in himself.

Many translations phrase the next sentence to read that his conduct will be shaped by the "laws" of that city within the wise
man. But Plato does not say that; he simply says that he will dwell
in that place. This point is important, because emphasis in *The
Republic* is never on laws; only late in life did he come to stress
the role of laws in the "second best" city. In the perfect city the
rational rule of an intellectual elite makes laws unnecessary (as
does the rule of the Confucian sage in classical China).

But there occurs in this connection a break in the whole argument which is the very Achilles heel of Plato's elitism. Socrates,
when asked how the "men of gold," the lovers of wisdom and
leaders of the city are to be found, admits that this is a formidable
question, and then, instead of answering it, suggests that only a
"royal" lie will enable the guardians to cope with that problem.
How could such lying ever be justified in an elite whose legitimacy rests upon their love of truth and wisdom? The process by
which political leaders are discovered is at the very heart of political life. All political thought revolves around it. The non-technical
nature of political activity and the rival notions of justice precipi-
tate the struggle for power and predominance. Plato, by admitting

that he has no true answer to this problem, concedes the bank-
ruptcy of his intellectual elitism. Yet, even so, a great step forward
had been achieved. Conventional elitism of prowess, wealth and
noble descent are devalued in favor of reason and moral conscience. In a sense the stage is set for medieval Christianity and
its belief in the spiritual sword as the companion and rival of
secular government. This is one of the great breakthroughs in the
spiritual history of mankind. After an age-old commitment to tribe
and community, a great thinker says: if you can not secure the
standard of what is right in the community you have to work it
out within yourself. It is the conscience, which Socrates called his
Daimonion. This "holy voice" will tell how to act rightly as it
told Socrates to take the poison and die because his fellow citizens
were of the opinion that he had violated the nomos. Only in this
act could Socrates prove that he believed in the nomos and that he
was not himself one of the Sophists against whom he had battled.

Let me make some concluding comments which go beyond
Plato. Here in this discovery of the conscience, the city within as
it has come to be called, is the philosophic root for what was later
developed in the Christian tradition. However, instead of the
philosopher seeking truth and justice by exercise of the rational
mind, the humble believer accepts revelation. The great drama
of this confrontation is found in St. Augustine. In St. Augustine's
City of God you will find an elaborate criticism of Plato and
Platonism. St. Augustine himself had been at one point a Platonist
and he described in the *Confessions* how he became dissatisfied
and could not abide them. The great accusation that he hurls at
Plato and the Platonists is that "ye are proud," proud to seek the
solution to the mysteries by rational inquiry, proud to discover
what is just by rational inquiry. The only way, says St. Augustine,
that these may be discovered is through Christian revelation,
through accepting the transcendency of the idea of what is good
and right. Through this shift, the elitism that is implied in Plato's
search for the rational guardian of the community is transformed
into the Christian idea of election and predestination. Justice in

Christian thought becomes the result of faith which works to produce good works. The reward is in heaven.

This idea of the reward which is in heaven was itself also found in Plato. Towards the end of his great discourse on *The Republic* he realized that there was something harsh and unconvincing about the development of his argument. He rounded out the story therefore with another one of his great myths, the myth of Er. The myth of Er relates how good souls are rewarded in heaven and evil ones are punished. In fact this myth of Er is a more detailed development of the idea of heaven and hell than can be found in the Bible where such references are quite short. If you ask yourself how it came about that the Christians developed such an elaborate notion as one finds eventually in Dante, the answer is in the myth of Er. In this myth there is a much more detailed portrayal of the eventual reward in heaven. This Christian attitude means, of course, the notion of election, of predestination and the acceptance of the humble believer as superior to the wisest of the wise. This egalitarianism was already found in the Old Testament and we shall come back to it. There intervened, however, a long period during which, in connection with the doctrine of the Charisma, the Christian Church developed the idea of the hierarchy. The hierarchy was not based on rational superiority but on charismatic superiority, superiority in the call to divine office.

Let me turn now to a conclusion, in a sense, for both of these lectures. Every argument in favor of a governing elite presupposes a knowledge of what is good and just for the community, and of who receives these truths. This is what Shakespeare had in mind when he wrote "Twice is he armed that has his quarrel just." But Josh Billings gave the pragmatic American answer, "and four times he who gets his fist in fust." The discussion that we have had leads beyond both of these propositions, the simple assumption that if one knows what is just one is in a better position to rule, and the latter one that after all it does not do you much good unless you are willing to assert your rights. I think modern man is much in the position of the later Plato. Plato suffered many disappointments. The greatest of these was his disappointment when he tried to realize his dreamed-of city in Syracuse with the help of the tyrant Dionysius. Plato has written of this in the Seventh Letter in terms which offer a gripping portrayal of the kind of experience which in our time has been put under the heading of "The God That Failed," the attempt to realize an ideal conception being frustrated by the recognition that politics goes on in its usual way.

I would like to conclude this lecture today with a passage from Burke who perhaps stands at the end of the period during which the Christian idea of a transcendent justice was a powerful one, a passage which Burke wrote when America was founded. It is a passage which makes one sad in the way in which Plato was sad when he wrote the Seventh Letter, full of disappointment and despair. It makes one sad because today we can no longer feel what Burke here expresses with that full confidence of the Christian rationalist of the eighteenth century. "There is one thing," Burke wrote, "and one thing only which defies all mutation but which existed before the world and will survive the fabric of the world itself. I mean justice, that justice which emanating from the Divinity has a place in the breast of every one of us and which will stand after this globe is burnt to ashes, our advocate or accuser before the great judge." In a sense you have here the assertion of the Platonic notion of justice. But you also have here in Burke its basic transformation as a result of Christianity. This idea of justice which maintains, he says, the fabric of the world and which emanates from the Divinity is no longer something that dwelt in the breast of the few who were seekers after that great end in the Platonic search after wisdom. Justice now dwells in the breast of every one of us. That is what happened when the Platonic doctrine was absorbed into Christianity. Out of it comes something that no longer contained the elitist notion except in the sense of a purely transcendent notion of the eventual judgment day before a Judge who really will know who knew what was right and acted accordingly, and who did not.

READINGS, SUGGESTED AND REQUIRED

Lectures 5 and 6:

REQUIRED READING:

PLATO, *The Republic,* tr. Cornford (Oxford).

SUGGESTIONS FOR FURTHER READING:

ROBERT DAHL, *Who Governs?* (Yale).

Justice, ed. C. J. Friedrich and John Chapman, Nomos VI (Atherton Press).

RONALD B. LEVINSON, *In Defense of Plato* (Harvard).

BENJAMIN LIPPINCOTT, *Victorian Critics of Democracy* (Octagon).

WALTER LIPPMANN, *Essays in the Public Philosophy* (Little, Brown).

JAMES H. MEISEL, *Myth of the Ruling Class: Gaetano Mosca and the Elite* (University of Michigan).

GAETANO MOSCA, *Ruling Class* (McGraw-Hill).

PLATO, *Statesman; Laws; Gorgias.*

Plato, Totalitarian or Democrat? ed. Thomas Landon Thorson (Prentice-Hall).

KARL POPPER, *Open Society and Its Enemies,* Vol. I: *Spell of Plato* (Harper Torchbooks).

ALFRED E. TAYLOR, *Plato: The Man and his Work* (Meridian).

7

Community and Order

THE PROBLEM OF COMMUNITY and order is at the very core of politics both in practice and in theory. Community and order, of course, like other key political subjects, have a dimension which reaches beyond politics into the social and personal sphere. Indeed, I intend in this lecture to make some comments linking the political aspect of community to the social and the personal.

When we talk about community and order we are confronted with something which Aristotle put at the very beginning of his great study on politics. Every kind of community, wrote Aristotle, aims at some good, that is to say has some purpose and the political, which is the highest community, has the highest of these purposes or objectives. There is a great deal of controversy about what this key sentence means, but there is very little doubt that he considered the *polis* a *koinonia*, that is to say a community. That is the kind of political order he was concerned about. The root of *koinonia* is *koinos*, which means common, just as the root of the word community is common.

One of the extraordinary features of our time is that the notion of community is much more generally used in politics than in the past. There is talk of the Atlantic community, the European community, the world community. The word community is bandied about to such an extent that one wonders whether this constant use of the word does not perhaps indicate some lack of community, some concern and worry at its absence. As you know, even in our educational institutions, there is now a great deal of talk about the need for human contact and the danger of alienation. When you inquire what is at the root of this concern, the answer is that there is a loss of community and that people who sense this estrangement do not like it. They miss the unity that was supposed to have been once part of their communal life. This may not be true for a traditional institution like Harvard, but at large and relatively new universities there is felt to be this lack of community. Even at Harvard there was felt, not long ago, this lack of community, but since then the University has built houses and a certain amount of communal living has returned.

Be that as it may, Aristotle was certainly right in thinking every community aims at some good and that the polis, the political community, being the highest of all communities, aims at the highest good. This statement directs attention to the essence of community, namely, that it is a group of persons who have values, interests and beliefs in common. Value is our more modern word referring to a "good." But the term "good" or "purpose" in Aristotelian understanding comprehends not only values, but also interests and beliefs. When Aristotle, therefore, says that the polis aims at the highest good, the most important purpose, what did he have in mind? What was involved? I think that what he had in mind and what was involved was, in a sense, the human personality. In Aristotle's view one could not be a human being without belonging to a polis. That is why he speaks of the human being as a political "animal." This is the conventional rendering of Aristotle's phrase; a more exact translation would be a "polis-inhabiting being." Man is somebody who needs a polis in order to live a truly human existence. Hence Aristotle is prepared to say that the polis aims at man's highest good. In other more limited communities such as professional and family, one also realizes important purposes, but they are surely far from being as necessary as the good provided by the polis.

It should be clear, however, that although the Aristotelian statement has been often repeated, we are not completely convinced by it. Indeed, if one reads Aristotle with a critical mind he is ready to reject this proposition. Why are we ready to reject this proposition? The reason is that most of us in the West would be inclined to say that another community, the church, pursues a higher aim than the political community. Most would say that here certainly is a community directing its attention to a more important and significant goal than does the political community. Some might even suggest that there are other kinds of conventional and created groups besides the religious that are concerned with more creative purposes than the political community. One might ask, then, how could this be the position of Aristotle? The answer is that the polis of which Aristotle speaks is not simply a political community. I mentioned earlier that the Greek notion of the polis was not merely that of a state, but also comprehended a church. The religious purposes and the religious aspirations of human beings were as much fulfilled in the polis as were the more strictly mundane concerns. This has even led some people to suggest that polis be translated not as state but as church-state, because it comprehends them both.

Once one recognizes that for Aristotle and the Greeks in general the polis did have this more inclusive understanding, it becomes more readily understandable why they should have thought that the polis pursues the highest of all objectives. What this highest goal might be relates to a problem we have encountered before: whether there is some kind of priority of goals or ends. Before we take this up, especially in relation to Aristotle, a number of general questions concerning political community need to be explored.

One of the most interesting is that of pluralism. It is the question of multiple membership, of membership in different communities. There can obviously be multiple membership in communities which are not specified as political communities. Most men belong to a church and to a profession as well as to a state. There is quite clearly multiple membership which begins with a family and rises to the intricate associational life of a modern industrial state. The question, however, which I would like to raise is more particularly the possibility of multiple membership in political communities. It is obvious that one cannot belong to several families, nor to several towns; one belongs to one. One may belong to two professions, but this is the exception rather than the rule. Neither can one belong to more than one nation, insofar as they are existentially considered. One cannot be at the same time both a Frenchman and a German; you are either one or the other. Nonetheless, we observe in the political sphere multiple membership. This fact is quite familiar to Americans because they are members of a federal union. The American is a citizen of a state, which makes him a member of one political community such as Massachusetts, Pennsylvania or Alabama, and at the same time he is a member of another political community, the United States. The same may be said of the German. He is a Bavarian as well as a German. Indeed Europeans today are beginning to think of themselves as both Germans and Europeans, or both French and Europeans. This illustrates that one can actually belong to three political communities. To the extent that Germans today are entering the European community, they are Bavarians, Germans and Europeans. If you consider the local community as politically relevant and consider it significant that you are a member of a specific town or a city as well as of a state or a nation, it is possible to enlarge this circle of membership to four or even five political communities.

How is this possible in the political sphere when the individual can only belong to one family or one profession or, as most people would say, one church? We might digress a moment to note that the oriental tradition is not as rigid as the western on the question of multiple membership. In the East the individual can belong to two or three religions at the same time. In the Orient religion is not so firmly organized as in the West. In such a tradition people can and do belong to two or more religions. Most people in the West, however, would insist that it is impossible to belong to two or more churches. One cannot be at the same time a Catholic and a Lutheran or a Catholic and a Presbyterian. The individual must choose and make up his mind whether he is one or the other. In the political sphere, however, this is accepted. How is this possible, is the question before us. The reason for this is very crucial for the understanding of the political community. In these other non-political communities there is usually involved one determinate purpose, goal, or loyalty. Political communities have many objectives. Added to this is the fact that in some communities, such as the family and the nation, belonging to a particular community may not be a matter of choice. One is a German because he is born a German. One is a member of a particular family because he is born a Saltenstall or a Friedrich. One cannot escape these communal ties because one cannot choose his parents or the folk to which he belongs. In the political sphere, however, the situation is quite noticeably different. If one does not like what is going on in Boston, he can move to Chicago and become a member of the Chicago political community. If one does not care for Alabama he can move away from there. Once the move is made to a new political community the individual might not like it any better, but for the time being he has exercised his choice. To a very considerable extent the political community today is a voluntary community. One makes up his mind to enter into one community or another. It can be voluntary because its goals are such that a temporary commitment is sufficient. Other voluntary communities, like a profession or a marriage (You may object that marriage is hardly voluntary; one is compelled by love to enter it. Still, legally marriage is voluntary today. It was not so in former times, when the family decided.) require a long, even a lifelong commitment. A political community does not. But there is another important reason for multiple membership in political communities.

As we mentioned before, something else is involved in political community which distinguishes it from other communities. A political community has many values, interests and beliefs; many goals are comprehended within it, unlike the dominant purpose found in other communities. The typical modern state comprehends many churches, many professions, many families. In all of these lesser communities the larger state does have some stake, although never so exclusive a stake as the subordinate communities which it embraces. For that reason it is possible for many different kinds of people having many different kinds or assortments of goal attachments and communal relationships to enter into a political community. The political community, so to speak, abstracts from the more specific and detailed goal attachments and offers a great variety of such assortments and relationships into which one can enter. For this reason it is possible as we know from the study of federalism, to "stack" a political community, to say a community will leave such and such activities to a local group, such and such activities to a regional group, such and such activities to a national government. At each one of these levels "stacking" of purposes, of goal or ends is related to community formations which are, however, defined by real political interests or goals. This is the heart of our argument about the pluralism of political communities. Many people would say that the great argument in favor of constitutional democracy is that it readily accepts this pluralism of political community formation and in fact it organizes the procedure which makes it possible for people to belong to various kinds of communities. Reversely, one of our objections to totalitarianism is that it tries to abolish such pluralism by producing a totalism of commitment to an inclusive ideology. There is, of course, a certain residue of pluralism left in totalitarian regimes. After all, the pluralism of the family cannot be totally eliminated. Still, the trend is away from it. Instead, the totalitarians espouse coordination, that is to say the central control of all groups and organizations by the totalitarian party and government and elimination of as many as possible of plural communal commitments. In a constitutional democracy, on the other hand, the trend is towards the recognition, acceptance and organizing of this plurality of communities. In a way, this was the argument between Plato and Aristotle. Plato was preoccupied with the problem of unity in connection with community. Aristotle thought this to be mistaken. There was in Plato's conception an excess of unity; what was needed was *comm*unity rather than unity. In pursuit of this objective, Aristotle sought a plurality of possible groupings which were united, to be sure, but not made uniform and wholly identical with each other.

At this point we can turn specifically to the problem of order. In discussing this issue I would again like to begin by introducing some very basic considerations for you. In political arguments the principle of order is often involved. There are some who insist simply that order must be maintained and they feel that with the incantation of this statement all argument is at an end. To such people this truth is self-evident and there can be no possible doubt that order must be maintained. Consequently whatever is necessary to maintain order is necessarily to be accepted and to be praised. Such an argument is based on the fallacious assumption that there is a self-evident priority of values, and that one particular value, namely order, is pre-eminent. All other values must be subordinated to this paramount value. I would heartily oppose such a position as I have just outlined. The first and most important thing to realize in connection with order in the sphere of politics is that like all other values it is relative to conflicting considerations of value, any one of which may in particular constellations take precedence over it. In other words, while we may all recognize that order is a value and that, other things being equal, it is desirable to realize order, upon reflection we must also insist that, while important, it is not all-important. There are other considerations of value which may be more significant under particular circumstances.

Let me ask you now to follow me into a more sophisticated argument about order. If we believe, as I reminded you a moment ago, that community is constituted by common values, interests and beliefs, we must realize next that these values, interests and beliefs are not stationary. These values, interests and beliefs constantly evolve, as I pointed out earlier, in the discussion on justice. They are subject to all kinds of changes, technological as well as other alterations in our existence. Because of this continual evolution of values, interests and beliefs, an effort must be made to give newer emergent values, interests and beliefs an opportunity to assert themselves. If this opportunity is given an element of disorder is obviously introduced into the community. If a situation is neatly arranged according to one set of values, as for example race relations in the United States were before that momentous Supreme Court decision in 1954, and a sudden change in values is introduced by saying that segregation is not compatible with the Constitution, then an element of very considerable disorder is introduced. There were quite a few good and legally-minded people who were very greatly disturbed and upset when the Supreme Court made that decision in 1954 and predicted that this would mean a lot of bloodshed. Right they were! It did mean a lot of bloodshed. The people who made that decision said in essence, this order is no longer compatible with the values, interests and beliefs of the predominant majority in America and the disorder involved in such a change is preferable to the injustice of order.

In this particular instance, as a matter of fact, the tranformation in the values was to some extent determined by outsiders, by the world situation. You know that our race relationship pattern here had evolved very slowly over the years. Still, if you compared the situation of the Negro in 1954 with the situation of the Negro in 1924, you would say it had very materially improved. It had materially improved for a variety of reasons, but the improvement was unquestionably there. It had not, however, improved rapidly enough to correspond to the very rapid transformation of the world outside the United States, where between 1924 and 1954 a great colonial revolution took place. All over the world, and more particularly in Africa, people who had been subject to the colonial rule of the British, the French and the Belgians and the other colonial powers had become independent. One result of their achievement of self-determination and self-government was the steady stream of African ambassadors, prime ministers, presidents and other dignitaries constantly arriving in Washington. There they were given state dinners, put into Blair House, in short treated like royalty. This meant that the colored citizen in the United States, still faced with a solid wall of discrimination, became increasingly embittered at his subordinate role. Here foreigners, colored foreigners, were treated in a way quite different from the way the American Negroes were treated. While the African Negro was given state dinners in Washington, the American Negro could not go into the corner drugstore and order a cup of coffee. I am giving you this particular illustration because it happens to be very much a concern at the moment. There can, however, be many other illustrations of a transformation of values and beliefs occasioned by forces wholly beyond the particular community in which they occur. Nonetheless they force themselves upon the community's attention.

Having once faced this phenomenon you begin to realize that there may not only be a value in order but even a value in disorder, a value in disorder which results from the fact that disorder may be related to value realization. I will give you another illustration in order to dramatize this for you in a way that I hope will enable you to retain this crucial issue and to bear it in mind when you encounter these problems on future occasions. Very frequently, as you have experienced in your personal life, there is a situation in which what seems to be order to one seems very much like disorder to another. This has incidentally led to the mistaken notion that order is very subjective, that it is merely in the mind of the beholder. This is quite untrue. The fallacy arises from the fact that there may be misunderstanding as to what constitutes order. You may, for example, go to my study at home and be struck by what would appear to you as appalling disorder. The whole place is strewn with papers and various kinds of manuscripts piled high. The same impression is created in the mind of my wife. But from my perspective this room presents beautiful order. To put it another way, it presents the value of disorder. At the present time I happen to be engaged in a particular task of revision and proofreading in which I need all of these different things lying on the floor. They must be readily accessible. It would be disastrous if they were packed away in drawers because it would take about four times as much time to do the job I have to do at the particular moment. The same is true of a workshop. A workshop will look different when a man is at work in it than on Sunday when the workshop is cleaned up. While the work is going on various tools have to lie around to be ready at hand. To put it in a very general and abstract way, a value is then being realized, a chair is being built. For this purpose the various tools needed have to be arranged in a way different than when the situation is one of no change, no creative development, no alteration or other kind of change.

With this background discussion about order and the value of disorder concluded, we can return to the problem of community. We have now equipped ourselves with a better basis for understanding and analyzing three great arguments about the nature of community that have occupied men thinking about politics ever since the days of Plato and Aristotle. I would like to present these three arguments to you and then give you what I believe to be the answers to the issues which this presentation raises. There is firstly, the argument whether community is a community of law or a community of love. This is the decisive argument between Cicero and St. Augustine. There is secondly the argument whether community is an organic community or whether the community is a purposive community. The third argument is in terms of whether the community is existential or whether the community is voluntary. These three arguments are inter-related and to some extent depend upon each other. Theorists in the history of political thought tend to line up either on the side of law, purpose and will, or on the side of love, organic community and existence. These then are the two great divisions in the interpretation of community.

What is the nature of the first argument over the community of law and the community of love? This distinction may be illustrated by the contrast between, on the one hand, two human beings who fall in love and raise a family and, on the other, two human beings who enter into partnership for the purpose of exploiting an invention in a business enterprise. These two contrasting kinds of community formation are, you might say, the primary ones. I do not think they are actually as different as they appear to be at first blush; indeed both of them are not only one but different mixtures of the two. I am inclined to argue, then, that every community is a community of both love and law. It may commence as the other; yet it may also develop correspondingly in the opposite direction at different rates of growth.

Let me now present the second pair of contrasts, the community as organic and community as purposive. This distinction is close to a German one which you often encounter in sociological writings, having been raised also by Burke and the Romantics. Ferdinand Tönnies coined the now popular distinction of *Gemeinschaft* and *Gesellschaft* which carries with it the contrast intended by the English adjectives organic and purposive. A community can on the one hand be constituted by the very life of the people who make it up. A characteristic organic community is a folk, a particular tribal group, or eventually even under modern conditions, a nation. Such an entity is organic in the sense that it exists regardless of any particular purposes that are being achieved or not being achieved. On the other hand, such an organic community will usually develop purposes which will also be involved in its organic existence as a community. Likewise I think you can say that when people are members of a business enterprise or of a university or of some other kind of purposive organization, they will also develop elements of an organic community relationship. This is simply because of the fact that when human beings get together, the fact that they are capable of sympathy produces organic relationships such as friendship and the like which reinforce the purposive element in that sort of community.

That last remark leads to the third pair of contrasts, the community as traditional, that is existential, and the community as voluntary. Locke, the father of classical liberalism, expounded the view that the political community is voluntary. Against such views, traditional doctrine had held since Aristotle that a real community is something that is there, a given, something that exists. It is something that comes into being by the mere existence of the people or persons who belong to it. The contrary position is that a community develops from wilful determination, from a choice which people make to enter into the community. Take for example the relationship of marriage, undoubtedly among the most familiar to all human beings. The relationship which develops between two human beings who fall in love with each other is something that exists, having a given reality all its own. As a matter of fact people who fall in love usually have that feeling very powerfully. They are convinced that their love has existence in itself and transcends any willful determination on their part; it is decided for them. That is why we have such lovely poetic phrases as that marriages are made in heaven. Such sentiments assert that there is an existential given which is the actual foundation of the community. There are, however, also elements of will and choice in this love relationship. If you insist on the dimension of will you can indeed say that the existential is really irrelevant. Love, you can claim, is just a subjective attitude in the minds of the people involved. Until they formulate out of this subjective reaction or impression something that can be called the "will," no community comes into being. My own views here are similar to the position I took in the two other cases; genuine community always involves both the existential and the willed. A community does not come into existence merely by existing, nor does it come into existence merely by being willed. Here, too, the two distinct elements have to come together and inter-act in order that a community may emerge.

I would like finally to develop for you two or three propositions with regard to political community that are important as implementation for what I have so far analyzed for you. It is very characteristic and significant that a political community usually has boundaries. This is not the case with all communities. We do not think, for example, of the community of marriage as one in which boundary is important. Such a community is not related to space. For the political community, however, boundary is very characteristic. Territorial boundary defines community. This principle must not be overstated, however. While it is usually so and while it is a characteristic feature of many political communities, it is not always present and there are political communities that are not defined by boundaries. Take, for example, the Jewish people. One of the most extraordinary political creations of mankind, it is a political community without any question, but it is not defined by boundary. Israel, on the other hand, an offshoot of the community called the Jewish people, is possessed of a boundary, albeit painfully possessed of a very difficult boundary. Thus it is desirable not to exaggerate this aspect, but to still recognize it.

The second point that I would like to make is that political communities tend to be structured. Not all communities are structured or organized. Part of this is a matter of size, but part of it is also inherent in the nature of political communities. You will remember the stress I have placed on political community being characterized by multiplicity of purpose, by multiplicity of goals and objectives. Well, such multiplicity of goal and objective insistently raises the problem of priority. What, for example, in any particular situation is the more important value to be realized? To determine this priority a community needs a procedure for reaching a decision. This need for decision in turn forces structure and organization. There must be argument on how the decision is made by which a particular value conflict is decided. Now, it is perfectly obvious that this tendency of political communities to be structured or organized grows as they in turn grow in size and in intrinsic complexity.

In this respect it has been interesting to watch the totalitarian dictatorships and more particularly the Soviet Union. The Soviet Union started out with an ideology which came out of Marxism and which looked upon organization in very simplistic terms, terms which minimized the problem of structure. As you remember in the *Communist Manifesto* the idea is conveyed that once the revolution is achieved there would be no need for any formal organizational structure. Everybody would be pleased with everybody else and there would be no administration of persons but only of things. Actually, as you know, the Soviet Union has developed a highly elaborate administrative structure. It possesses a vast bureaucracy with a greatly differentiated structure. Organizational adjustments are continually attempted in the hope of more nearly achieving the kind of purposes sought by the revolutionary society. In the course of time some of these aims have proved incompatible, so that a choice between them has to be made. This is very characteristic for a political community and it has some relation to the size of the community and the complexity of its level of civilization.

The third proposition that I would like to mention at the end of this lecture today is the fact that political communities always develop myths, symbols and utopias. Some thorough-going rationalists do not like to face this fact. They think it ought to be possible to build a completely rational community. I do not believe that this is likely to happen. In any case, if we look over the history of mankind we find that wherever there have been political communities there have been myths, symbols and utopias. This fact is very deeply linked to the nature of political communities. Because communities have this complex nature highlighted by the six elements of love, law, organism, purpose, existence and will, there are any number of situations which are too complicated to be set forth for practical purposes. The symbol, however, is the great tool for simplifying complex relationships. The symbol most readily at hand is, of course, the flag; but the constitution is likewise a symbol. Associated with the symbol there grow up myths which are also abbreviations. One of the most familiar myths in America is the founder myth. In this country everybody grows up knowing certain mythical details about the Pilgrim Fathers and how they came to these shores. Everyone also knows that later in Philadelphia the fathers of the Constitution drafted this great charter. Historical scholarship has sought to cope with these myths, to try to sift out what is really true from the mythical. The enormous vital necessity of these myths is demonstrated, however, by the fact that in spite of all such scholarship people go right on maintaining these myths. Sometimes they even recognize them as myths. Still they go on telling the same story because that story has a vital significance in maintaining the idea of the community's existential dimension. Perhaps only a word more is needed about utopias for I have mentioned utopias before. A political community, much like the individual human being, needs a certain amount of hope in order to exist. Hope in a political community embodies itself in a utopian conception as to what the community should be like. In the United States and in some other countries we aspire to be a democracy. This notion of constitutional democracy is, however, only a guide. Most people understand that it cannot be realized exactly as it is conceived. It is a lodestar that we can follow. This is the essence, then, of utopia, a projection of aspirations into the future which are necessary in order to maintain the purposive vitality of the community as it was originally conceived.

Here is one final thought relating the concept of community and the concept of order to what I have told you about the value of dis-order. A community while based on common values, interests and beliefs, presupposes dissent if it is to be a vital community. A community that has no dissent, that contains no element of radical disagreement from its commitments, including the commitments to myths, symbols and utopia, is not likely to be a community of any considerable vitality. In other words, we always have to envision as the limiting danger of both community and order, the order of the graveyard. The graveyard is completely ordered because absolutely nothing happens there. Of course even in the graveyard a disturbance occasionally occurs. Somebody dies and the grave digger appears and digs out a new hole. The beautiful order of the graveyard is disturbed because there is now raw soil with wilted flowers on top of it. So you see that even the graveyard is a vital part of something that is going on. My point is the danger of over-stressing the common in the values, interests and beliefs. If you over-stress order in the structuring and organizing of the community, the community becomes self-defeating. It becomes, as I say, the order of the graveyard, the community of the dead. In a living community in which the purposes are related to evolving values, interests and beliefs there will always be vigorous dissent.

8

Aristotle, Philosopher of the Political Community

A MONG ALL THINKERS who have contributed to an understanding of political community, Aristotle is foremost.
He made this topic the very center of his political
analysis. To be sure, Plato too had been deeply concerned with
community and order. But in Plato, the focus was primarily on
justice and nomos. In Aristotle's *Politics* the opening sentences at
once state his preoccupation with community. "Every polis is a
community (*koinonia*) of some kind. . . ." And why is there
this concern with communal aspects of politics? The emphasis on
the political community in Aristotle's writings on politics is closely
linked to his stress on happiness as the purpose of human existence, its true *telos*. I shall deal with this Aristotelian hedonism
more fully further on. It is related to his most characteristic
philosophical doctrine and discovery of the philosophical notion of
telos or the "end" as the most central concern of the search after
wisdom. This telos transcends Plato's notion of ideas and more
particularly Plato's idea of the good. I might at this point say a

word about the relationship of Aristotle and Plato. This has been a topic of considerable interest to philosophers and the historians of philosophy for many a generation. There are essentially two views. One would have Aristotle as merely a second best Plato who tried to reproduce the teachings of his master but without much success. The other would, on the contrary, contrast Plato and Aristotle as worlds apart. For this view the great question is how to choose between Plato and Aristotle. This question is, of course, tied up with the problem of what actually is the difference between Plato and Aristotle. On this problem there is a common view which depicts Aristotle as an empiricist and Plato as an idealist. I do not think that this is a good way of describing the differences between the two men. Aristotle was much closer to Plato than this distinction would suggest. For Aristotle was not an empiricist in the modern sense of the word even though he was concerned with what human beings did and what they were striving for. He was, however, also a deductive philosopher expounding a basic conceptual framework in terms of which these experiences are approached. Aristotle, too, is an idealist, believing in norms and deductive truth. But Aristotle is, in contrast to Plato the poet-philosopher, much more the scientist-philosopher. This appears in their way of writing which is strikingly different. Aristotle writes about politics much the way most of us write today. That his book resembles the kind of book you usually read is a testimony to the great intellectual influence of Aristotle. He has shaped the mind of Western thinkers and scholars and how they go about dealing with matters intellectual, including the writing of books. Plato, by contrast, is quite untypical. He writes dialogues—a form of discourse not often employed for scientific exposition. Rarely does Plato include an initial statement putting his position as Aristotle puts his position at the beginning of both the *Politics* and the *Ethics*.

One final point on the subject of Plato and Aristotle. Because it has been difficult to find in Plato's works exactly what Aristotle says are Plato's views some have claimed that poor old Aristotle just did not understand Plato. I have always felt that this is a most peculiar position to take. Aristotle, who had been associated with Plato for over twenty years as a pupil and collaborator in his Academy, would obviously write of Plato's views in a more knowledgeable manner than would one who merely read Plato's works. Nor would Aristotle bind himself solely to what is found in Plato's works in speaking of the views of Plato. Indeed, I think that considering the enormous intellectual capacity of Aristotle, we have every reason to assume that when Aristotle says that Plato was of a certain opinion, his judgment is entitled to a great deal of respect as an interpretation of Plato's views because it represents a more intimate view of them than can be gathered by reading Plato's own works. This is reinforced by the fact that, as we saw, Plato wrote that he would never put on paper what he really thought. But Aristotle heard him. It is silly, therefore, to cite what Plato wrote against what Aristotle, his pupil, said Plato thought. Aristotle did after all hear from Plato directly what Plato thought, as contrasted with the writings that are available to us. So much, then, for the interesting problem of the relationship between the two great Greek thinkers.

Let me return to the central Aristotelian notion of the telos. Aristotle's stress on the telos or the end of things as the ultimate basis for the understanding of things is clearly visible in the opening sentences of the *Politics*. These opening sentences are very much the key to all that Aristotle has to tell us on politics.

Let us examine these passages with some care. "Every polis is a community of some kind, and every community is established with a view to some good; for men always act in order to obtain that which they think good." This is the great Jowett's translation, slightly adapted. Another British scholar, the late Professor Ernest Barker of Cambridge University, has made a rather different one, since he liked to make a lot of commentary, interpretive embellishments and elaborations; he was also fond of using contemporary terms which are anachronistic in the context of Aristotle's writings, such as sovereignty. More particularly, he translated the first sentence of the *Politics* quite misleadingly, by rendering *koinonia* (see above p. 105) as association and inserted "as observation shows us"—something which Aristotle does not say at all. The genuine Aristotle speaks quite apodictically, and proceeds to argue deductively about community. He sets forth his basic teleological approach to politics which makes him assert at the outset that all men act with a view to some apparent good—a proposition which implies a teleological, or as we incline to say, functionalist view of man and his government. The communities which he forms are similarly in the first place "directed toward some end," that is to say to be understood in terms of their telos. How does Aristotle continue the argument? We read: "If all communities aim at some good, the polis or political community, which is the highest of all, and which embraces all the rest, aims at good in a greater degree than any other, and at the highest good." The Greek word for "highest" is here the superlative of *kyrios* which means lord, ruler and the like, and hence the argument really is that the community which is the most lordly and on top of all other minor communities, such as families, brotherhoods and guilds, is *therefore* also aiming at the most lordly, most important good. Apart from the pure verbalism involved, it may well be questioned whether the fact that the political community rules the other communities makes their values the most important. But Aristotle unquestionably asserts it, on the basis of his analogical reasoning. He thereby lays the foundation for his later insistence upon the need of such a community by any man seeking self-fulfillment and happiness.

There is, in many translations and interpretations, found a propensity to render the superlative of *kyrios* as sovereign. But the notion of sovereignty in its primary modern meaning implies the notion of being "free from law" (*legibus solutus*) as Bodin has put it in the sixteenth century in developing the concept of sovereignty, and such a notion is quite alien to Aristotle, as it had been to Plato. That a community is highest in the sense of having no superior does not at all free it from the law. Even if we interpolate that such a polis community is the most powerful, or even the strongest, it still is presumed to operate within the nomos, the law and custom of the existing order of things. In Aristotle's original text there is thus none of the legalistic political terminology conveyed by the word sovereignty. He is merely offering a descriptive proposition which asserts that a polis community is above the other communities as a matter of fact. From this established matter of fact, Aristotle then proceeds to argue as we have just shown.

A bit later he claims that men by their very nature are inclined to live in such communities. His Greek expression that man is a *dzoon politikon* means that he is a "being living in a polis," just as we might say that bees are hive-dwelling animals or that cattle and deer live in herds. But Aristotle does not actually say that man is a "political animal" as so many translations and commentaries have it. The idea that man is an animal is not very Aristotelian, though he is equally far from denying man's relation to animals. As Professor McIlwain wrote, Aristotle distinguishes no less sharply between man "who alone has reason" and mere animals, as he does between animals "who have a soul" and plants who have not. For the polis is for Aristotle "the final stage in the development of man's nature." It is man's telos to become fully man only within the context of a political community. We must, however, bear in mind that "political" is used in a rather specific sense by the Greeks which is at once more particular and more comprehensive than our usage (see p. 79 ff.). The political is only what "belongs to the polis." It excludes empires, but it also includes the religious dimension. The polis is concerned with both the ecclesiastical and the secular sphere. In common parlance today, the term political refers only to secular activity. Yet one cannot say the polis is the state *and* the church because it is neither. This differentiation which is so characteristic for our western development had not occurred in Greece, as it has not in many primitive communities to this very day.

If we bear in mind this religious connotation of the *koinonia politica,* the Greek political community, we come face to face with the problem of the relation of politics to ethics. Aristotle dealt with this in another very important work, the *Nicomachean Ethics.* The *Nicomachean Ethics* has a very definite relationship to the *Politics* which we are studying. "They supplement each other by

treating a common field according to different aspects" according
to one of the great Aristotelian scholars of our time (McKeon).
Both works are concerned with the happiness of man. The *Ethics*
seeks to determine the inner psychic and moral conditions of happiness, while the *Politics* is concerned with the outer, the communal conditions of happiness. Both are inquiries into the greatest
good or happiness. For this reason both works are part of one
episteme, one system of knowledge, or understanding, or science
in the broadest sense. Ethics and politics are closely linked to each
other. It is no surprise, then, that at the end of the *Ethics* we find
a kind of a program for the *Politics.* Aristotle there gives an outline of the *Politics.* This has, incidentally, created another set of
long lasting headaches for scholars. The text of the *Politics* that
has come down through the ages does not precisely correspond to
Aristotle's outline in the *Ethics.* If you remember that both the
Ethics and *Politics* are actually based on lecture notes of students,
and consider your own lecture notes in connection with my lectures, you will readily understand why the outline and the finished
product do not precisely fit each other. In any case, I think the
general indication of the outline is quite clear and it does provide
the link between the two works. If, then, the polis is the perfected
community, it is so because it has reached the limit of what Aristotle called self-sufficiency or *autarkeia.* We still use the word
autarchy but we usually mean it in an economic sense. In Aristotle
autarkeia is not an economic phenomenon but primarily an ethical
and psychic one. He means self-sufficiency in the sense of being a
rounded self. This self-sufficiency is a characteristic of the polis
community and of those who compose it. Relating this proposition
to a contemporary argument, self-sufficiency prevents alienation.
The self-sufficient man is the opposite of the alienated man.
Through his communal existence, which the polis provides, man
attains such self-sufficiency. Community came into being for the
sake of mere existence, *tzēn,* but it continues to exist for the good
life, for the *eu tzēn.* Let us hear Aristotle himself on this point.
"When we come to the final and perfect association, the community, formed from a number of villages, we have already

reached the polis, an association that may be said to have reached the height of full self-sufficiency. Or rather, to speak more exactly we may say that while it grows for the sake of mere life, it exists for the sake of the good life." (*Politics* 1252, B 27-end)

This notion of self-sufficiency should be explored in relation to two problems, treated by Aristotle. One is the problem of size and the other is the need for diversity. The problem of size is hardly ever discussed today in an age of big national communities. We treat the size of nations more or less as a fact of nature. We do not dispute whether one nation like the Greek is too small or another like the American is rather large, or the Chinese much too large. It seems to us a given biological fact how large nations are. But when the discussion concerns a newly founded, voluntary establishment, corresponding to the polis notion of the Greeks, such as a university, the argument about size is a very live one indeed. There has been much debate recently about what the optimal size of a school of higher learning ought to be, which is natural enough when new universities are to be established. Many people are not at all happy about the multi-versity that has been announced as the wave of the future. Similarly, in Greece they argued about the size of cities. Not only Plato and Aristotle, but a number of other men whose ideas Aristotle discusses, had views on the optimal size of cities. One of these who had been an advisor to Pericles on the building of the harbor of Athens, the Piraeus, had suggested about 10,000 citizens as right. This would mean, with women, children, slaves, foreigners and so on between 80 and 100 thousand inhabitants. Such a size seemed too large to Plato who in *The Laws,* a late dialogue, advises 5040. Aristotle objects to this number as too large. Being sober and inclined to relate his arguments to experience, he speaks of the round figure of 5000, since he was convinced that it was too large, anyhow, and cared little for Plato's astrological and numerological speculations. The Platonic body of citizens would mean 40 to 50 thousand inhabitants. Aristotle does not give a specific number, but suggests that experience with well-governed cities provides a basis. But presumably he had one to two thousand in mind. The underlying thought in both Plato and Aristotle was that too large a size disrupts the communal life and undermines the political order. As Aristotle puts it: "Law is order, and good law is good order; but a very great multitude cannot be orderly." And he concludes the argument by saying that "the best limit of the population of a polis is the largest number which suffices for the purposes of life, and can be seen well as a whole (*eusynoptos*)." (*Pol.* 1326) The standard of members of the citizenry knowing each other had already been urged by Plato. For then they can talk with one another. At the present time a similar argument over size is heard in New England in connection with the question of how long the old town meeting type of government is viable. There are some people who say as long as there are not more than 1000 voters and others say not more than 2000, and others say 500. It is the same argument found in Aristotle. Beyond a certain number it is impossible to engage in meaningful confrontation. In such cases, where the size of the town meeting no longer enables people to encounter one another, the open meeting is being replaced by a representative body.

The second problem related to self-sufficiency of the community is the degree of unity. Here again Aristotle criticizes Plato. Aristotle accuses Plato of over-emphasizing unity. Aristotle's views are very much in line with today's attitudes. In his opinion a community presupposes that its component parts have a measure of self-sufficiency, of *autarkeia*. These parts must exist by themselves and have a life of their own before they can form a community. A community must never be a perfect unity; it must also be a diversity of autonomous and self-sufficient members. These views prompted Aristotle to criticize bitterly Plato's community of wives and property. In such a collective situation, wrote Aristotle, people cease to be persons because they no longer have a sphere of their own. They are totally absorbed into the community. This would be true whether the components of a community were persons, families, villages, or what have you.

In light of these views it is surprising that Aristotle's thought did not evolve towards the notion of a federal union of many cities, a political idea very much in the air in his day. The Achaean league was soon to come into existence. One might have expected Aristotle to suggest that several autonomous self-sufficient polis could form a unified community, a federal union. This idea is not forthcoming, however, for Aristotle the polis provides the limits (*peras*) of self-sufficiency. It is not feasible to achieve a greater self-sufficiency than is possible in the polis. Central here is this matter of size. When you go beyond the polis, there is no longer any possibility for confrontation, the immediacy of community is lost. Very different is the outlook in Europe today, where it is the wider community of Europe which many dream of as an alternative to the national state. And yet, is there not also an element of Greek thinking in the lingering doubts of those who, like General de Gaulle, doubt the possibility of such a European community replacing the national communities?

One reason the Greeks could seriously discuss such a small citizen body as Plato and Aristotle favored is, of course, their acceptance of slavery. Though we cannot discuss this institution in any detail, I want at least to mention it. Aristotle undertakes to justify slavery insisting that there are men who are slaves by nature. It seems to me one of the classic cases of a circular argument which proves nothing and simply repeats the premise from which it starts. Be that as it may, all these men who perform the menial tasks could be excluded from the community; they were not part of the polis. This sentiment was, as you know, very much shared by the noble and self-sufficient gentlemen in this country and England, down to the early nineteenth century.

I would like now to turn to a discussion of the *Ethics* and to cite a few passages from it. I think that Aristotle's thoughts on the central focus of human existence and, hence, the foundation of community, are more clearly revealed in the *Ethics* than in the *Politics*. The crucial passages for Aristotle's views are found in the very beginning of the work. The opening sentence of the *Ethics* reads: "Every art and every science reduced to a teachable form, and in like manner every action and moral choice aims, it is thought, at some good; for which reason a common and by no means a bad description of what the chief good is, is that which all things aim at." Here you have a general discussion of what we would today call the problem of value. Aristotle proceeds on the basis of this very general characterization to make the following observations a little further on: "And now resuming the statement with which we commenced, since all knowledge and moral choice grasps at good of some kind or another, what good is that which we say politicae aims at?" Remember, when Aristotle says politics it includes religion. "Or in other words, what is the highest of all the goods which are the objects of action? So far as name goes," answers Aristotle, "there is a pretty general agreement. For happiness both the multitude and the refined few call it, and living well and doing well they conceive it to be the same with being happy." In orther words happiness, the highest good, is something which is apparently empirically based. Aristotle says that happiness is what most people would describe as the highest good. Aristotle's assertion is in line with modern social psychology. In a sense he is saying go and ask one of these pollsters to survey opinion on the highest good. The result of the survey would be general agreement on happiness. "But," Aristotle adds, and here comes the philosopher with his problems, "about the nature of this happiness men dispute and the multitude do not in their account of it agree with the wise." Aristotle then enumerates all the different ways in which human beings might define happiness or might define value for themselves. But ultimately, out of all this review of various motivations there emerges Aristotle's conviction that happiness is "always desirable in itself and never for the sake of something else. . . . We choose it always for itself." (*Pol.* 1097a) What this means is that happiness is the ultimate value. It is not instrumental but intrinsic. To be sure, we choose honor, pleasure, intellect and in fact every excellence for themselves, too. But this we do, because such activities of the soul make a man happy, because they provide him with self-fulfillment. That is why we would choose each of these even if no other result were to follow, but we seek them all also because of the happiness they bring. That is to say that they are in a sense intrinsic, yet not fully so. But no man chooses happiness with a view to honor and these other values, but strictly for itself.

In the following passage Aristotle sets off this notion of happiness from possible confusing notions, some of which have played a great role in political thought. First of all he disposes of Hobbes, and Hobbesian principles long before the Englishman came along. Aristotle insisted that mere life does not give happiness because such life is plainly shared by man even with vegetables and we want what is peculiar to man. We want to set off man. (*Pol.* 1098a) Here Aristotle is the humanist above all. He goes on to say that also the life of the senses does not bring happiness, because it is manifestly common to horses, oxen and every animal. Aristotle thus arrives at what he considers the true source of happiness, namely man's rational nature. I would like to cite for you the famous passage in which this discussion of the rational nature of man culminates. "If all this is so, then human good turns out to be a working of the soul in the way of excellence." A working of the soul in the way of excellence! In view of the importance of this conclusion, I cannot restrain myself from giving you the Greek original, much as I dare say it will just puzzle you: *to anthropinon agathon psyches energeia ginetai kat'areten.* This is the famous formula which says better than the translator what Aristotle wanted to say. One of these Greek words, *energeia,* contains the root word which is "work," *ergon. Energon* means to be "at work." Happiness, therefore, consists in the mind and soul of man at work. This is the supreme and distinctly human form of happiness as contrasted with the many other things which are also pleasurable and nice.

If Aristotle ended his discussion of happiness here he would be one of the many philosophers and religious sages to whom most people would reply: "I do not want to live just the life of the mind. I like to have a pleasant life too." But Aristotle is a much wiser man than most. He rejects the famous saying of Solon that man can only be called happy after he dies; for "is it not absurd to call a man happy only when he is dead, especially when we say that happiness is an activity?" Happiness is the best, noblest, and most pleasant thing in the world, but "we need external goods as well." For noble deeds require a certain freedom from want. "In many situations we use friends and riches and political power as instruments." We also need good birth, goodly children, and beauty, and a man is not likely to be happy if he lacks these. "Happiness seems to need this sort of prosperity." (*Pol.* 1099b)

Here you clearly see the humane aspect of Aristotle. He does not doubt that the life of the mind is the source of the highest happiness. But Aristotle realizes that other things are also necessary. Man cannot be in a very unsatisfactory condition with respect to basic human needs and still enjoy in the fullest sense the activities of the mind and soul. Aristotle is of the opinion that the community must provide the necessary conditions for the life of the mind. The contemplative, or more aptly described, active life of the seeker after wisdom is made possible by his being a member of the live and active community that provides all these other things such as property, family, and friends, that are necessary conditions for the fulfillment of one's existence. Aristotle speaks for a kind of individualism which would have the political order, the community, exist for men and not men for the political order. Man is meant to live in cities, but they must be well-ordered which means that they should be stable. In order to achieve such stability, all extremes should be avoided. As in many other fields, so also in political science Aristotle is forever searching for the middle road, the mean or *mesotes,* what the French call the *bonne mesure.* For the social order in a well-arranged city this calls for a broad middle class of men who are neither rich nor poor, but solid sound citizens. We do not know his vast canvass of Greek cities, covering well over a hundred of them, except for the study of the *Athenian Constitution,* but we may surmise that Aristotle could offer empirical evidence for this desirability of the middle class.

Related to this stress on the middle class and stability is Aristotle's dislike for change and more especially revolution. Any political order, he seems to feel, is better than its violent overthrow, except possibly tyranny. But then tyranny is short-lived anyhow. Broadly speaking, his famous theory of revolution is that when the political order fails to correspond to the distribution of property and hence of the class structure, tensions arise which will eventually lead to revolution. Arguments over justice are at the heart of them.

In order to avoid such catastrophe, Aristotle develops a model constitution. It is a mixed form of government in which all citizens have some share in the government. He even states the basic principle of constitutional democracy that on everyday practical problems the many in their majority are apt to be wiser than the learned few. But one must not turn the government over to them, as radical democracy does. Rather, the many should contribute their share in the popular assembly, while a council of seniors will restrain them, and the actual administration will be left to one or a few. There are hints here of what was to become the doctrine of the separation of powers in modern constitutional theory as shaped in the seventeenth century by Harrington, Locke and others. Basically, Aristotle's view is dominated by the concern for stability, however, and the modern notion of organized political change is entirely lacking. Yet, it was a projection, and when Polybius many generations after Aristotle adapted the model of a mixed constitution to an interpretation of the Roman republic, he provided the basis for later employment of Aristotle's view.

I would like to conclude this lecture with some comments on Aristotle's fate in the subsequent history of political thought. Professor Bury in his great Greek history makes the following comment: "It is not an overstatement to say that there is no one to whom Europe owes a greater debt for the higher education of her peoples than Aristotle." It is doubtful whether this statement is quite correct in this general form. Nevertheless, I think it is true when restricted to the political sphere. If Bury had claimed that there is no one to whom Europe owes a greater debt for the higher *political* education of her peoples than Aristotle, I would think it entirely true.

The most important of Europe's students of Aristotle's politics was Thomas Aquinas, the great scholastic. Aristotle's influence before the work of Aquinas, however, also deserves mention. After the fall of Rome Aristotle virtually disappeared from Europe. To be sure this was not a total disappearance. There were always some remnants of his thought present, but on the whole his writings disappeared. The Arabs having taken over his thought from the Greeks in the east, preserved the Aristotelian learning throughout Europe's dark ages. His thought returned to Europe via the Arabs and via Spain in the late twelfth and thirteenth century. Because of his doctrine of happiness, and its emphasis on the communal conditions of happiness, Aristotle made a tremendous impact on European thinkers. Quite a number of people were ready to go over entirely to his doctrines. This posed a problem for the Catholic Church. There obviously were very serious conflicts between Aristotle's natural philosophy and the transcendental theology of the Christian Church. Thomas Aquinas' great achievement was to produce a kind of concordance of Aristotle's political and other philosophy with the Christian tradition. Aquinas succeeded so well that with this restatement of Aristotle, he shaped the entire thinking of the later middle ages. In founding the great tradition of scholasticism, he developed a framework for political thought as well as political action. The most important development from the point of view of Christianity and political thought is that Thomas accepted Aristotle's teaching on the naturalness of political community. He agreed that human beings naturally liked to enter into association with each other. He accepted the fact that in this association men reached a species of happiness. Aquinas was unable, however, to adopt the pagan notion that the political community was the final community because in the intervening centuries the Christian separation of church and state had occurred. Nonetheless, Thomas transcended the Augustinian and Pauline tradition which looked upon the political community as something quite low, merely committed to the preservation of peace, and merely concerned with providing a corrective for the intrinsic sinfulness of men. Rejecting that tradition, Aquinas proclaimed with a new optimism and a new naturalism, that human beings should live in political communities, that this was their natural way. This was not merely a matter of sin, but a matter of their self-fulfillment. Thomas put it another and more theological way: God wants human beings to live in political community for their own happiness. In the creation of his great synthesis, Thomas changed Aristotle somewhat and in a sense the essential Aristotle had to be rediscovered in later years by careful scholarship. So tremendous became the influence of Thomas Aquinas that for 300 years men read Aristotle as if he had been a Christian. You may remember that Dante put Aristotle into a very favorable position because of the significance he had acquired in shaping the Christian tradition.

At the heart of Aristotle's great legacy is the idea that the political community is the essential condition for human happiness, that human happiness must be defined not in strictly spiritual terms, but needs for its implementation a recognition of its more ordinary requirements and finally that only in this way can order be achieved.

READINGS, SUGGESTED AND REQUIRED

Lectures 7 and 8:

REQUIRED READING:

ARISTOTLE, *Politics,* Books I–VI, tr. Barker (Galaxy). *Ethics,* Books I and V.

SUGGESTIONS FOR FURTHER READING:

Aristotle, ed. Werner Jaeger (Oxford University Press).
Aristotle, ed. Richard McKeon (Random).
JACOB BURCKHARDT, *History of Greek Culture* (Ungar).
SEBASTIAN DEGRAZIA, *The Political Community* (Phoenix).
Community, ed. C. J. Friedrich, Nomos II (Liberal Arts).
MASON HAMMOND, *City State and World State* (Harvard).
RICHARD KOEBNER, *Empire* (Grosset).

LEWIS MUMFORD, *The City in History* (Harcourt, Brace & World).

ALFRED E. TAYLOR, *Aristotle* (Dover).

ERIC VOEGLIN, *Order and History,* Vol. 1: *Israel and Revelation;* Vol. 3: *Plato and Aristotle* (Louisiana State).

9
Power and Authority

MANY STUDENTS of political science claim that this is the central topic of political studies. They would consider it wrong that we come to power only in the latter part of these lectures. Not beginning with such a discussion is seen as a typical traditionalist oversight by the modern behaviorist convinced that power is the heart of politics. Harold Lasswell, one of the leading political scientists of our generation, put this position in a rather dramatic way in a title to a book he wrote in the mid-thirties, *Politics: Who Gets What, When and How.* This stimulating little essay on the subject of power dealt with the question of who possessed political power. But you can see by his formulation that power can well be and has indeed been, a subject that goes a good way beyond the field of politics. The power of agents, for example, can be a power quite different from political power. What we are concerned with here is of course political power, not power in the general sense.

There is one famous definition of power which does characteristically go beyond the field of politics, although it occurs in one of the great theoretical studies of politics, namely Thomas Hobbes' *Leviathan.* In the tenth chapter of that famous book there occurs a definition of power which says that "power is the present means to obtain some future apparent good." There are various teasers or traps in this definition, such as the introduction of the word "apparent" which frees the author from discussing whether the good is really good as long as it appears good to the one who seeks to secure it. This definition of power obviously extends beyond the strictly political. It could include, for example, wealth, because wealth is certainly a present means to obtain some future apparent good. Other things such as physical strength or attractiveness are also means to secure some future apparent good. They are all parts of power in the broadest sense, but they are obviously only a part of political power. In that respect, then, the definition is too broad. But it is also too narrow in that it fails to take account of the fact that power is often not a possession, a kind of substance, that is, which somebody has and can use against somebody else. Frequently it is a give-and-take that rests upon a relation between two or more people and is properly described as a relation rather than a possession. Hence, these two kinds of power have been spoken of as substantive and relational power. In modern writings on power there is a tendency to see power predominantly as a relation rather than a possession. Yet stressing the relational dimension is not necessarily a good way out either, for it is clear that power is often a possession. When one is elected to an office, he receives with that office certain stated powers to have and to hold like possessions. They may be enjoyed, abused, wielded, and so forth. Any kind of office-holder acquires a certain amount of such power with his office. The power of that office may be greatly enhanced if its holder is skillful in utilizing his power in relations with others. It may also be considerably reduced by unskillful use of power. Anyone who has observed elected officials come into office has noticed that some are capable of immediately making the most skillful use of their given possession of power in relations with others and thereby greatly enhancing their total power. If the setup is democratic as in this country such increase in power is much more feasible than it would be in a less democratic country (though by no means excluded in an autocratic one, as the history of monarchy shows). This is clearly seen by a comparison of Johnson with Kosygin and Brezhnev. Johnson at once upon stepping into the presidency utilized the given resources of the office with exceptional know-how and practical skill. In this manner he has considerably increased the actual power which the office gave him when he succeeded Kennedy. On the other hand we are much less certain with regard to Kosygin and Brezhnev what the actual power situation is. It does not seem likely at the present time that they have the same power that Khrushchev had at the height of his rule. Both of them, of course, have been put into a context in which a skillful use of the power placed at their disposal may increase or decrease their total power. I will return to this subject when I talk about authority, which is closely linked to this augmentation of official power.

If we cannot satisfactorily define power the way Hobbes and others have done because such a definition is both too broad and too narrow, the question still confronts us: what is political power? How can we effectively characterize it? I myself lean towards a rather behavioral characterization or description of power. I would suggest that power can best be described in terms of followership, by saying that somebody has political power over another or several others if these others can be observed to follow his preferences and do what he would like them to do rather than what they would prefer to do themselves. This "rather" is a tricky word, however. Skillful use of power produces the tendency in people to want to do what the leader exercising power desires them to do. We thus see that converting coercion into consent is very much connected with the skillful use of power. In short, power is not merely a matter of command, as claimed in a great many writings on politics. The customary tendency is to identify power with the ability to give commands. This is, no doubt, an important part of power, but it is not the whole story. A great deal of power is of a very different sort. There is first of all the power connected with persuasion. A persuasive man has a considerable amount of power unrelated to any ability he may have to give commands. Then there is also influence, a very important form of power; it is usually, in fact almost always exercised without any command. One man influences another man in the field of politics by getting him to act the way he would like him to act without any overt command. For this reason it has been said, and with good grounds, that influence is hidden power, a more or less invisible form of power. A great deal of the power exercised by pressure groups and propagandists is of this hidden sort. The effort to control the exercise of such hidden power merely consists in prescribing that it must be made public. When we make a law in the United States obliging foreign agents to register and to disclose the source of their funds we are using precisely this instrumentality of publicity to reduce the hidden power possessed by these agents. The law does not forbid people to be agents of the British, German or Russian government. It merely says if you are such an agent you must register this fact and you must also disclose where you are getting the money. This is done because it is quite clear that once it is disclosed that Mr. Miller is an agent of Moscow and that he receives $10,000 from the Russian government, many people will be rather cautious in dealing with Miller. Indeed some might absolutely refuse to. In this way the law has quite effectively reduced Miller's influence.

This is the next basic question the student of politics must ask: What are the sources of power? From what I have said it is already apparent, to some extent, what the answer will be. The source of power that is a possession is primarily coercion. When an officeholder acquires a certain amount of power, he acquires the ability to coerce. The source of relational power, on the other hand, is to a great extent consensual or cooperatiive. A leader who seeks to develop a new organization will very largely depend upon consensual or cooperative power. He will organize his followers by arousing in them a desire to go along with his own objectives and purposes. Now there is a certain sophistry which enters the discussion at this point and which has created a great deal of confusion in political analysis and political theory. This sophistry sees no difference between coercion and consent because consent is produced by the power of persuasion. This, it is argued, is nothing more than the power of putting oneself forward in the best way, which is, after all, some kind of psychic coercion. In other words persuasion, it is argued, actually involves manipulating the person who is being persuaded. If this is so, then what really is the difference between consent and coercion? It is true that coercion and consent are not mutually exclusive. At the same time, however, there is a difference clear to all of us which is very important for politics, there is a difference, surely, between the man who sticks a pistol into our belly and says "give me your purse" and the man who swamps us with letters of one sort or another and secures the same amount from us as the robber by persuading us that it is wonderful to support some organization. Perhaps these are both forms of coercion, but somehow we feel differently coerced in the two different situations.

This brings me to another point, quite important in connection with coercion. There are clearly different forms of coercion. One can distinguish physical coercion, economic coercion, and psychic coercion. Even within the field of these three forms of coersion there are differences. If, for example, the man who tried to persuade me to support some organization tells me the truth and thus appeals to what I genuinely believe, I will not be coerced in a technical sense. By misrepresenting the situation in a propagandistic way he exercises manipulative power which deceives me and prevents me from knowing what really is going to be done when I part with my dough.

At this point I would like to call your attention to one more basic issue, the contrast between rule and rulership and power and the wielding and handling of power. Bluntly stated we can say that there is a difference between a leader and a ruler. A leader is one who is in a direct dynamic relationship with his following. He has little coercive power, his power being a product of his ability to persuade his followers. A ruler is a very much more formal exerciser of political power. This is due to the fact that in ruling their realms, rulers exercise an organized and structured power. Such power is, in modern societies, organized usually by law, that is by constitutional charters. The Constitution of the United States, for example, says that the President has certain specified powers. This basic law, therefore, structures his power. He has no other powers unless he is able to persuade others to go along with his preferences. If the President succeeds in being very persuasive with Congress so that Congress will do his bidding, he acquires in addition to the power the Constitution gives him, a substantial part of the power the Constitution gives to Congress. In this way the President greatly enhances his power. Thus in all highly developed political orders there is a constant interaction between leadership and rulership and for that reason also between structured and unstructured power.

At this point I reach the important and difficult problem of authority. Authority has been much less generally recognized as a key aspect of politics than has power. The great theorists of power said little about the distinct problem of authority. You should by now be reading two of these theorists, Machiavelli and Hobbes. Machiavelli is really the writer who first put the problem of power on the map, so to speak. He was primarily concerned, perhaps as a result of the time in which he lived, with power in the brute sense, of the successful deployment of violence. The Italian Renaissance was a very violent time and in Florence politics was a dangerous profession. Authority is a different matter and Machiavelli paid little attention to it. I would urge you not to confuse authority with power, although this is frequently done. The two words are incorrectly used interchangeably. This is in part due to the way in which people speak of "the authority" meaning actually the power-holders or the office-holders. Since we cannot ever completely clarify common speech, we will have to live with these confused usages of our basic terms. But for a precise political analysis, the kind of analysis needed for a deeper understanding of politics, it is important to separate and distinguish authority from power.

Authority is not a kind of power, but something that accompanies power. It is a quality in men and things which enhances their power, something which creates power but is not itself power. It might be rather useful to go back to the origin of the word. On the whole, you know, I do not bother with these word origins because most of the time they are not very revealing. Often, as a matter of fact, they are a source of error. In the case of authority, however, we are able to learn a good deal from the origin of the word. *Authority* derives from the Latin word *auctoritas*. It was associated with a particular political institution, the Senate. The Senate of Rome, derived as you know from *senex*, the old man, contained the elders of the political community as it does in so many primitive communities where the elders are organized into some kind of counsel for advice. This Senate had a special contribution to make to political decisions. When a law was made in this ancient constitutional republic, the people gathered in their popular assemblies and made the policy decision. The Romans, however, were by tradition a conservative people, deeply and continually influenced by religious considerations. Hence they did not feel sure that a popular decision was quite enough. The people ought certainly to say what they *want* to do, but there still existed the problem of whether the particular decision was agreeable to the gods. Was it really something that *ought* to be so decided? This was related to another consideration. Was the popular preference in keeping with what was customarily done in Rome? Could it be fitted into the traditions of the Roman Republic? These religious and traditional questions were answered by the Roman Senate as it ratified or rejected the assembly decision. We have, by the way, in the function of this Senate something that resembles that of the Supreme Court of the United States. The Supreme Court is much more rationally elaborated, but it too evaluates the decisions of the legislative assembly in the light of the great tradition embodied in what we call the Constitution. This Court, too, is called upon to decide if something is or is not agreeable to the Constitution, and hence to the tradition of the American Republic. The Romans did not work with a written constitution and thus had a more difficult time resolving these questions. The tradition being tied to religion made the task even more complicated. The old men of the Senate were asked to settle the issue and when they said "yes, the law also pleases us; we are in agreement," it was said the law had acquired *auctoritas*. It had acquired authority because the decision of *will* on the part of the popular assembly had been enlarged by a decision of "reason," as the old men reflected upon the wisdom of the legislation in terms of tradition and religion.

This analysis leads to another very important point. Although it may appear so at first glance, authority is not opposed to reason but is actually the embodiment of reason. This reasoning, however, is not reason in the sense of mathematical demonstration, nor in the sense of Cartesian logic which reaches a necessary conclusion from a given starting point by a rigorous process of ratiocination. It is rather reasoning in the sense in which we speak of reason when we are concerned with expedient matters that involve value judgments and interests. In such circumstances we ask: Given this interest, given this value, given this belief, what is the right solution to your problem? Authority is the capacity to justify by a process of reasoning what is desired from the point of view of mere will, desire, or preference. Let me elaborate this somewhat by straying from the field of politics. Consider for a moment the authority of a scholar or a professor. When you sit here and listen to me, occasionally writing down a note, you take a great deal of what I say on authority. You are quite willing to let it be, if Professor Friedrich says so. Now you really ought not to from a Socratic point of view. You should make sure that everything is exactly the way Professor Friedrich says it is. You might begin by exploring the authorities to which he referred. After this lecture, for example, you should immediately rush to the library and get out Lasswell's book to see whether I have misrepresented Lasswell which I may well have done. If you should be so ornery a character as to read Lasswell and would discover that Friedrich misrepresented Lasswell, then surely his authority would decline with you. You might even say, "I do not trust old Professor Friedrich any longer; he deceived me about Lasswell, why should I believe what he says about Machiavelli? Perhaps I ought to go and read Machiavelli!" Authority you see is something rather mysterious. Consider now the parallel case of a doctor. When we go to a doctor we all accept his authority which, when you think of it, is very curious. For the predictions doctors make are often wrong, even in very serious situations involving the death of the patient. I am sure you all know cases, as I do, where death had been predicted, but did not occur, just as there are others where death overtakes a man who has just been told that he will be all right, provided he takes certain precautions. The authority of the doctor rests upon his knowing *more* and having *better* reasons, even though his knowledge is defective. Indeed, where knowledge is complete and there can be no question, as in elementary mathematics, authority plays only a small role.

In all situations where uncertainty and contingency play a significant role, on the other hand, the question of who has the better basis for judgment becomes vital. This is true not only in medicine and the law, but more particularly in politics. Authority may be great or small, but it is always a factor. LBJ tells us that we must step up the war in Vietnam, and the majority of Americans go along, although some people express doubts that the proposal is sound and advise against it. Why do most people go along? They say that this is such a complicated matter that they do not know enough about it to have a judgment of their own. The President, however, has access to a great deal of information and advice from people who know all about Vietnam and Communism. Hence they prefer to abide by his judgment and accept his authority.

Is there any similarity, then, between the authority of the doctor, the professor and the President? Is the meaning of authority roughly comparable or even the same in politics as in those other areas of human relations? I would answer: yes to both these questions. In all of these examples the man who has authority possesses something that I would describe as the capacity for reasoned elaboration, for giving convincing reasons for what he does or proposes to have others do. Let me make clearer what I mean by that. If we accept the authority of the professor on the platform, the doctor in the office, or the President in the White House the reason we do so is that we have a conviction based on a good deal of experience. We feel that if we could ask them to elaborate and if the time permitted, they would have a lot of good reasons for having spoken and decided as they did. In the end we might not have arrived at the same conclusion, but we accept the fact that there is not enough time. In any case, the man whose authority one accepts has "his" reasons. He has the capacity for elaborating, with many good reasons, upon what he has put forward as the right action to take. In the political community such reasoning often relates to the values, interests and beliefs prevalent in the community. That reasoning is, in other words, dependent upon a community of such values, interests and beliefs.

This reasoning about actions in terms of values, interests and beliefs is obviously something that is subject to change. Now you can understand why there often occurs a curious augmentation and decline of authority. I would say, and I think many would agree with me, that when Johnson came into the Presidential office his authority was not very large. A great many people felt grave dismay. Many who had been enthusiastic about Kennedy and believed in his leadership saw his successor as little more than a ward politician. This was the reaction of nearly everybody although there were some, most noticeably members of Congress, who felt quite differently about Johnson's abilities. Gradually, as his time in office has passed, Johnson's authority has increased. It has increased on a variety of grounds, all of which are related to the fact that people saw as this man got into action that he possesses a quality which Americans value tremendously, the ability to succeed. When Johnson proclaims, "I want such and such a thing in legislation," lo and behold, and contrary to what we had come to expect, the Congress goes along agreeing to just that. This success has made a deep impression upon a great many people, greatly enhancing Johnson's authority. Therefore a lot of people are inclined to look to Johnson with confidence when it comes to difficult issues. They feel he will somehow work it out, somehow figure out a way. There is confidence on the part of the American people that Johnson possesses the capacity for reasoned elaboration. One finds similar phenomena in other countries. Take for example the case of Adenauer. Adenauer was elected chancellor by one vote; many claim it was his own. It is clear then that at the beginning of this tenure he had nothing but the ill-defined coercive power of a chancellor, which was considerable, but by no means approximated what he eventually had. He succeeded, however, in building up an enormous authority and even today when Adenauer no longer has the office of chancellor, he is at times still called the secret chancellor of Germany. The authority he acquired carried beyond his office because the capacity for reasoned elaboration he possesses is a personal quality which transcends the explicit powers that go with the office.

We can on the other hand also observe the decline of authority. Take the case of Khrushchev. We will not know the facts on this case for a long time, but I think there is little doubt that at some point before October, 1964, there must have set in a sharp decline in the authority of Khrushchev. In his formal power nothing changed. There was only one indication of change in 1964 when several articles in Soviet military journals criticized Khrushchev in the sharpest possible way as the destroyer of the defensive position of the Soviet Union. Evidently, not only did Khrushchev lose his authority in the armed forces, but doubts as to his good sense, his capacity for reasoning soundly, arose in his immediate entourage. This the later accusations against him revealed. By speaking of his impetuosity, his recklessness and similar traits and habits, his successors intimated his loss of authority. Similar dramatic revelations have accompanied the sudden fall of Sukarno and Nkrumah. Such events will help explain why I think it so important that the student of politics separate authority from power. In the field of authority one is able to observe phenomena that are outside the sphere of power. In this connection I might point out to you one other thing. The loss of authority is often most noticeable in the case of aging leaders. Khrushchev and Sukarno are cases in point. What is really involved here, when leaders age? A leader continues to cherish the values, interests and beliefs of the time when he came into power. In the meantime the world has not stood still. People, the citizens of a political community, change, partly in response to a changing environment. More important is that their values change and with their values their interests and beliefs. This is in part a question of generations. There occurs a continuous alteration of the human material which supports political power. As the younger generation comes to the fore there may be such a difference between the values of the leadership and the values of the followership that this capacity for reasoned elaboration although continuing as an individual capacity ceases to be politically viable. The reasoning which might have made perfectly good sense in terms of the old values does not make good sense in terms of the new values. On great occasions this lag leads with fantastic suddenness to the total collapse of political power. Like an empty shell a political system disappears. These are usually instances where not only individuals but whole systems have lost their authority and could not maintain their rule with merely the resources of coercion, since their persuasive power is in eclipse. The authority which must go with government for it to be effective for any length of time is gone. Examples of such sudden and total collapse are the French situation before the great revolution of 1789 or the Russian situation before the great revolution of 1917. In both cases one finds systems in which the people associated with the system had completely lost the capacity for reasoned elaboration, because their values, interests and beliefs were so utterly unshared by the community at large. In such a situation they were bound to disappear, and so they did.

IO

Machiavelli and Hobbes—
Theorists of Political Power

MACHIAVELLI AND HOBBES are certainly among the thinkers most worthy of study in the history of political thought. They were both preoccupied with the problem of power, but in rather different ways. In my last lecture I gave you Hobbes' definition of power and a critical evaluation of it. Machiavelli does not offer a definition of power; he never defines. As a historian and man of affairs, he uses the words in common parlance as he finds them. It makes reading him easier at first, but harder when you want to be sure of what he has in mind.

There is a famous saying of Lord Acton which you may have heard cited: "All power," he wrote to a friend, "tends to corrupt, and absolute power corrupts absolutely." The quotation is somewhat torn from context, but anyway: is it true? No, I should say. Some men are undoubtedly corrupted by power, and particularly so, if their power is "absolute." (Power never is really absolute, by the way.) But other men are ennobled by power. The possession of power heightens their sense of responsibility. Lord Bryce and others have commented, e.g., upon the fact that rather ordinary men, when elected to the American Presidency, have at times become greater than they seemed before. We have had some recent examples of that.

The notion that power tends to corrupt is nonetheless deeply rooted in our Christian tradition; it is one of the politically most important legacies. The doctrine of the two kingdoms or cities is a part of that tradition, as is the belief that if all men were true Christians, no government would be needed. The tendency of the New Testament is anti-organizational and anti-power for that reason; remember the admonition of Jesus that his kingdom is not of this world. Power, it seems, is something for worldly people. True Christians are people concerned with the salvation of their souls. Their virtue is a humility which is ready to "offer the other cheek." Hence they are indifferent to the threatening and somewhat sinister realm of power.

To all such notions, Machiavelli was radically opposed. He was the foremost writer to reject this Christian bias as irrelevant to politics. He proclaimed with bold frankness that all the medieval notions about a Christian prince were but dreams: "My intention is to write something of use . . ." he wrote in his handbook for princes, for "many have imagined republics and principalities which have been seen or known to exist in reality; for how we live is far removed from how we ought to live." Therefore, any man who has to wield power had better be realistic about how to use it, lest he bring disaster upon the state. "Therefore it is necessary for a prince . . . to learn how not to be good. . . ." Machiavelli, in accordance with this outlook, put power and its dynamics at the center of his political thought. Writing in the sixteenth century, Machiavelli was by no means without predecessors in his concern with power. His writings are in the spirit of the Italian Renaissance which reinforced by Humanism had resuscitated the thought of the ancients, and in the sequel had become more and more worldly and pagan. Characteristically, Machiavelli was inspired by these works, but more by the historians than by the philosophers. Only historians, he felt, had explored the reality of politics. Machiavelli rejected what he considered the idealistic tradition of Plato, Aristotle and Aquinas and replaced it with a hard headed description of concrete reality as he found it in Tacitus, Polybius, Thucydides and indeed Titus Livius, upon whom Machiavelli built his most comprehensive work, the *Discourses Upon the Ten Books of Titus Livius on Roman History*. Machiavelli was quite unsophisticated about the historical accuracy of these historians, one has to concede, however, that although we are now much more critical of what these antique historians reported about Romulus and Remus, Tarquinius, and the other greats of Roman history, these findings little affect Machiavelli's arguments. If we revise the *Titus Livius* of tradition in terms of critical historical scholarship, most of the arguments of Machiavelli would remain as well supported as they were by the literary Livius with whom Machiavelli worked. The reason for this is easy to discover. What Machiavelli was primarily concerned with in the writings of the classical historians was what you might call the heart of the matter rather than specific details. The heart of the matter was simply the ebb and flow of power.

Machiavelli's reaction to power was certainly not Lord Acton's conviction that power corrupts. This attitude is, by the way, still endemic in American thinking on politics. It is clearly present, for example, in the popular characterization of the politician as some kind of a scummy character, dubious at best and someone whose company one ought to avoid lest one get involved in a corruption scandal. This type of thinking Machiavelli totally rejects. For him the seeker of power and the manipulator and wielder of power were the acme of humankind, the men who had a chance at the greatest of human achievements. Machiavelli, following the tradition of the ancients, was convinced that the political order was the quintessential setting for the display of genuine virtue. Machiavelli's conception of virtue was similar to that of the Romans and the Greeks. In Rome *Virtus,* the source of the word virtue, strongly carried the meaning of the first syllable, *Vir,* man. *Virtus* implied the qualities of the fighter and warrior, those of a virile individual. This notion of *Virtus* is evoked in the American tradition by the image of the red-blooded American which is usually set against the virtues of the do-gooder, the Christer, the fellow who wants to help other people. It is this image of the manly warrior, who asserts himself and fights for his rights that Machiavelli believes requires the political order for its most effective self-realization.

Machiavelli has rejected the Christian notion of virtue for the secular and political values of the ancient world. He is willing to recognize religion, but primarily because of its value in strengthening the political order. Once again it is Rome which served as his model, Rome where the prevailing religion was a state religion which supported the political order. A kind of idealized picture of Roman polity is the inspiration for Machiavelli's image of the best political order. Machiavelli's nostalgia for ancient Rome left him with burning hatred for the Christian church, which meant for him the Roman Catholic Church. This Roman Church, wrote Machiavelli, had been the corruptor of Italy; it had made the Italians bad. It had corrupted them, made them *cattivi, cattivi* being a strong expression in Italian, carrying with it the implication of evil, something rotten to the core. He reinforced this sentiment by suggesting that if by chance the seat of the Pope should be transferred from Rome to Switzerland, a country distinguished by a considerable amount of virtue, the Swiss would be corrupted within two generations and would become as rotten as the Italians.

This attack on Christianity and on its striving for secular power is an aspect of Machiavelli's thinking which is to some extent a heritage of the Renaissance and its exalted esteem of things ancient. Such sentiments found in a number of writers in the fifteenth century are an important complement to Machiavelli's political glorification of state and power. For Machiavelli, an official of the Florentine republic during its relatively brief libertarian and constitutionalist period, the state was a work of art. Indeed the great Burckhardt tells us that Renaissance man saw the state as the greatest of all works of art. The Italian Renaissance, as you know, was the great age of human adoration of art. The celebration of Giotto's success in painting in perspective is comparable to the way Americans celebrate a great baseball player, or conceivably a movie actress. Giotto was praised for having achieved a new form of expression in painting. The same appreciation held, of course, for sculpture, architecture and the rest. Machiavelli, in keeping with the prevailing mood of his era, indicated that the greatest of all artistic creations of man was the state. The greatest of all arts was that of building a political order. Now Machiavelli thought of state-building very much in Renaissance terms. It is an activity on the order of Brunelleschi's, the builder of the Duomo in Florence who had amazed his contemporaries by artistically solving the great technical problems involved in building the vast cupola of the Florentine cathedral. If you see the cathedral you will note that it was both a technical and artistic achievement. For Renaissance man the building of the state was also a technical as well as an artistic achievement. One very crucial aspect of any technical achievement is a mastery of the materials worked with. One must posit the limit of the materials and what can be done with them in order to be a great artist. The materials used in the great work of art that is the state are, as Machiavelli saw it, human beings. One must not deceive himself about the nature of human beings or he will be like a builder of a cathedral who treats stone as if it were wood, or wood as if it were some kind of flexible material.

In looking at his human material, Machiavelli was a "realist." His view is generally considered a very pessimistic one. He describes men in rather uncomplimentary terms. This negativism is tempered, however, by a very considerable dose of optimism. This same human being who, generally speaking, so deplorably lacks *virtù*, the quality of greatness, is also capable of superb achievements. For besides the mass of ordinary men, there is the hero, the superb man. Like Nietzsche's superman, Machiavelli's great leader, the founder of the state is a unique person endowed with superb *virtù*, virtue. When building or remodeling a political order such a great man is capable of infusing his virtue into the entire citizenry. These miserable creatures which human beings usually are or tend to become when not properly guided are thereby transformed into patriotic citizens, capable of sacrifice, self-exertion and all the other patriotic virtues. But man's natural tendency is to lose that virtue. Gradually he succumbs to corruption and once again a great man must appear to reestablish the commonwealth. So there exists a natural cycle, not quite like that in the Greek philosophers, but more an alternation between good and *virtù*-filled republics and various degenerate governments.

One should not misunderstand Machiavelli's attitude in this connection. It is most important to realize that he was extremely hostile to Caesar. He has been misread by many people as one who would welcome a Caesar capable of reestablishing the power of the state. But Machiavelli clearly rejects Caesar and Caesarism. He described Caesar as one of the worst men in Roman history. Why was Machiavelli of this opinion? Caesar, he felt, had destroyed Roman freedom. He had destroyed the venerable Roman constitution instead of regenerating or recreating it. Someone who destroys a constitutional order is to be despised even though he be a strong man and a powerful man. His attitude toward Caesar reveals that there is a certain inconsistency or in-built contradiction in Machiavelli's thought which becomes evident when one compares his *Prince* with his *Discourses*. In *The Prince* he clearly seems to imply that at certain desperate turns rather anti-libertarian characters such as the Italian Condottiere, whom Cesare Borgia much admired, can reconstitute the Florentine Commonwealth, or even unite Italy, as he hopes the addressee of the work, the Medici Prince, might do. In his more reflective work, *The Discourses*, however, he makes it clear that once this task of re-unification or of re-establishing the power of the state, is accomplished, such a leader cannot be considered the great builder of a true state unless he transforms this reconstituted community into a constitutional order. This explains Machiavelli's admiration for a figure like Solon, the famous Athenian legislator, who departed from Athens for many years after he had given it a new constitution, for fear that if he stayed he might become a tyrant. Machiavelli fully approved of this course of action. He advised his statesman-reformer to follow this path as contrasted with the wrong actions of such as Caesar.

I would like to mention one other point of great importance in connection with Machiavelli's attitude toward power, the notion of reason of state. When one is confronted with the tasks government poses, be it the major secular task of building a political order or the minor but nonetheless important task of maintaining a political order and operating it effectively, there are continually situations in which one is confronted with the problem of acting rationally, in the sense of acting successfully. There is in all of Machiavelli's writings a persistent anti-Christian and indeed pagan preoccupation with success. Such success is the opposite of any kind of self-sacrifice in terms of other-worldly concerns or of goals and causes for which men will give up their lives. To Machiavelli anyone who proposed to die for a lost cause was a fool, and not worthy of consideration. This emphasis on success of operations leads Machiavelli to a kind of emphasis on expediency, a purely pragmatic rationality in connection with politics. It is this rationality which the term "reason of state" is meant to designate. "Reason of state" is a pragmatic rationality that is not concerned with whether the goals being sought are intrinsically reasonable or not. Its concern is purely with the question of how to conduct operations that lead to a successful conclusion. In this connection the claim is frequently made that Machiavelli was an expounder of the doctrine that the end justifies the means. From what I have just said to you it must be clear, however, that this cannot be the case. Indeed, the sentence "end justifies the means" does not even occur in Machiavelli's writings. It is found in your translation but it does not occur in Machiavelli's original text. The translator was so sure that this was what Machiavelli must have meant that he translated a sentence which in Italian reads "every action is designed in terms of the end which it seeks to achieve," as the very different kind of notion that the "end justifies the means." The reason Machiavelli does not expound the view that the end justifies the means will be quite clear. He is not at all interested in the justification of means. For Machiavelli the means are the means rationally designed for achieving an end. Justification is unnecessary. The problem of justification arises only when one must match such rationality in terms of the needs of the situation with some conflicting moral, religious or ethical conviction. This is precisely the problem that Machiavelli eliminated by saying that the organization itself, namely the state, is the highest value beyond which there is no limiting standard.

On turning from Machiavelli to Hobbes, one encounters a very different kind of person and a very different political climate. One and a quarter centuries after the writing of *The Prince* Hobbes published his major works. In 1642 there appeared *De Cive,* a kind of summary treatment of the problems of the *Leviathan* and in 1651 the *Leviathan* itself was published. Hobbes wrote in the midst of the great English revolution. His writings thus fall historically within the context of the Puritan's challenge to English constitutional tradition and the concurrent monarchical effort to transform this tradition. Consequently the social context of Hobbes' England was that of a traditional monarchy challenged by revolutionary democratic forces. The Italian Renaissance, on the contrary, saw a multiplicity of absolute rulers of the Italian city-states fighting with each other. This incessant warfare created discontent and weakness so widespread that all Italy lay open to foreign invasion. Not only were the historical situations in which Hobbes and Machiavelli operated quite different, so too were their personalities. Hobbes was very unlike Machiavelli. He was a cloistered man writing out of the ivory tower. Extremely difficult as it may be to construct a complete ivory tower, Hobbes nearly succeeded. He managed quite well in avoiding personal involvement such as getting a wife or joining an organization or holding an office. He also avoided all forms of academic involvement such as most writers on politics who become members of a university faculty are committed to. Such involvements preclude an ivory tower existence and inevitably involve practical politics. Even a university faculty is not devoid of politics. There is a true anecdote told about Woodrow Wilson which illustrates this point rather nicely. When Wilson, who had been a professor and president of Princeton, became governor of New Jersey, a rather tough fight occurred at one time in the Governor's Council. One of the professional politicians turned to Wilson and said, "Well, Professor, you didn't realize what you were getting into when you let yourself be elected governor and left your academic cloister over in Princeton." Wilson smiled and said: "My dear friend, this kind of politics is child's play compared to academic politics." Hobbes did not involve himself in this sort of thing. He preferred his ivory tower. On occasion he was the companion of some great lord and lived in his manor house, but primarily he was preoccupied with his thinking and writing.

At one and the same time, however, Hobbes is *the* philosopher of power. Much more than even Machiavelli, Hobbes is centrally concerned with the problem of power. In *The Leviathan,* which you have been reading, he describes the life of man as a "perpetual and restless desire for power after power unto death." Hobbes saw the human condition as a ceaseless striving for power. Incidentally, these views entitle Hobbes to be looked upon as the philosopher of his age. The seventeenth century in general is charactrized by a recognition of and a preoccupation with power. But Hobbes' writings on power display, in a sense, a deep love/hate ambivalence. It is clear that he detests this very realm of power which he thinks is the central one with which human beings must cope. Hobbes, then, bases his political thought on a very different conception of human existence than does Machiavelli. Whereas Machiavelli is in one sense pessimistic regarding the ordinary man, but optimistic regarding the exceptional man, Hobbes is pessimistic through and through. His pessimism extends to all human beings. There is a famous chapter on equality in *Leviathan* in which Hobbes challenged a long tradition which some cherish to this day. He denies there that any real difference exists between human beings. He is the egalitarian par excellence. Perhaps, he concedes, there might be some slight differences between people in physical strength and mental ability, but on the whole they are not significant enough to alter the basic equality of men. Most human beings are like most other human beings and they are all pretty miserable!

One indication of their sorry and fearful lot is the ultimate proof of their equality: the equal capacity of all individuals to kill one another.

On the basis of this conception of human nature, Hobbes developed what has been rightly described as his mechanistic materialism. This mechanistic materialism can be summed up best by one of Hobbes' own sentences, "life is but motion." Such a view places Hobbes firmly in the tradition rapidly developing in Europe after 1600 which we label the scientific revolution. Mechanics became the central preoccupation of intellectuals from Galileo to Newton. Hobbes undertook to fit politics into mechanics by proceeding on the premise that life was but motion. In the interesting introductory two pages of *The Leviathan,* which I recommend to your reflection and thought, he tried to develop the argument that life was mere mechanism, something akin to a watch with its various components. It could be assembled, analyzed, and understood like any other machine. This notion of Hobbes marks an important milestone in the history of political thought. Essential to Hobbes' theory is the devaluation of reason, the great mother of so much of political philosophy from Plato down to Hobbes. For Hobbes reason is mere reckoning. It has nothing to do with reflecting upon really deep issues of wisdom as it did for Plato and Aristotle. Reason is now merely calculating, adding and subtracting, as he sometimes puts it.

What are such unhappy and miserable men reckoning about? What are they calculating? Hobbes answers that man's basic motivation is the fear of violent death. There is no *summum bonum,* no highest good, but there is a *summum malum,* a highest evil. The highest evil is to leave this life before one's time as a result of violent death. It is important to note that Hobbes speaks of *violent* death; it is often stated that Hobbes speaks merely of the fear of death. This is not true. Indeed, the fear of death produces a quite different kind of political philosophy. After all we all have to die. The general fear of death puts one into a metaphysical mood, leads one to speculation about the afterlife and immortality. It is the source of much religious thought. In Hobbes the stress is on the fear of violent death. His concern is not religious, for this violence results mostly from hostile human beings who attack and deprive one another of life, the most important of all values. There are other rival motivations like greed and the desire for glory, but these are merely incidental to the basic motivation, the fear of violent death. It leads to the basic law of nature. According to Hobbes there is a law of nature, in the same sense that the law of gravitation is a law of nature, which is that all human beings are seeking security and to avoid violent death. It is about this that men reckon, that men calculate.

It is on this foundation that Hobbes offers his striking argument on how the state comes into being. You remember that in Machiavelli the superior individual who knows how to accumulate and manipulate power builds a state out of the recalcitrant material that are men. Hobbes' account is quite different. All these miserable men who are quaking in their boots because they might lose their lives by violent death gather together and make a contract with each other to escape from their miserable condition. In order to accomplish this, what must they do? They must write into the contract, "I agree with you and you agree with me that we will submit ourselves to someone else whom we will both allow to be the holder of absolute power over us. This person we shall call the Sovereign of our commonwealth." The Sovereign of the absolute state comes into existence because those subject to him have agreed with each other that without him their life is intolerable. In this connection I want to cite one more famous passage from Hobbes which gives some indication of his extraordinary stylistic power. In this passage he describes what would be the situation if frightened men did not agree on a sovereign power above them. It is clear from this passage that there is in Hobbes' mind a notion of something besides bare subsistence as constituting values for human beings. This citation is from chapter 13 of the *Leviathan* and occurs in the context of Hobbes' discussion of the state of war. "The condition prior to their entering into the contract, the state of nature, is a condition of war of all against all, a condition of universal and general war with the constant threat of violent death. Whatsoever therefore is consequent to a time of war where every man is enemy to every man, the same is consequent to the time when men live without any other security than what their own strength and their own invention should furnish them withal. In such condition there is no place for industry because the fruits thereof are uncertain, and consequently no culture of the earth, no navigation nor use of the commodities that may be imported by sea, no commodious buildings, no instruments of moving and removing such things as require much force, no knowledge of the face of the earth, no account of time, no arts, no letters, no societies, and which is worst of all, continual fear and danger of violent death and the life of man—solitary, poor, nasty, brutish and short." This sentence always reminds me of the African student who describes Hobbes' state of nature as "solitary, poor, nasty, *British* and short."

This description of the state of nature is really the heart of the Hobbesian position. The fear of violent death is its most characteristic feature, but we must not forget that there are other unpleasant aspects of the state of nature. Hobbes did recognize that the lack of industry, letters and arts also led men to dislike their natural state, but they could not compare to the central crucial value of effective survival. This alone made it a law of nature for all prudent men to seek peace; peace defined in the organization of political society.

There is a good deal more that one can say on this score, but I would like to single out one other important ingredient in Hobbes' political theory, his theory of representation. Hobbes is most keen on having one man be the recipient of the power of all the other men that come together to form political society. He is an Englishman and writing in England so he always adds after his description of the unitary sovereign the words, "or a group of men," but it is obvious he does not truly believe in this concession and makes it simply for the sake of the readers. One reason why he is so preoccupied with having one single ruler is derived from his notion of representation. In chapter 16, Hobbes writes that a group or multitude of people cannot be one except through the single person who represents them. The one who represents all is the creator of the political order because only in this way can a group of people become one. This is why I suggested that Hobbes' casual acceptance of "maybe also a group of men" was merely rhetoric. It is contradicted by this emphasis on the multitude being represented by one in order to become one. Machiavelli, it might be noted, has very little to say about the crucial problem of representation. In this respect, as in so many other important ones, Machiavelli was still solidly in the tradition of classical antiquity which was not concerned with the problem of representation.

So far I have developed for you these two writers' attitudes toward power. It remains to say a word about their thought on authority. On this score I would be inclined to put the rather extreme proposition that neither Machiavelli nor Hobbes understood the phenomenon of authority. In some ways their defectiveness as political thinkers is revealed in this failure to understand the issues presented by authority as contrasted with the issues raised by power. It is very interesting in this respect to contrast Machiavelli and Hobbes with Plato and Aristotle, particularly Plato, because he was preoccupied with the problem of authority and in turn neglected as unimportant the problem of power. What seemed to Plato to be of primary importance is what I tried to develop for you as the problem of authority. The lack of interest in this problem of our modern pair of writers may be explained to some extent by the fact that both Machiavelli and Hobbes were preoccupied with the problem of how to organize power and how to bring the state into existence. They were concerned with the origin of the state, rather than the operation of the state and the maintenance of a political order. What is essential to note is that only when one is concerned with the maintenance of a political order does the problem of authority move into the foreground. As has been rightly said, you cannot sit for long upon bayonets, so you cannot for long maintain an effective order with mere brute power; you must add to it this other element of authority which I explained to you last time.

Now, what accounts for Machiavelli's and Hobbes' emphasis on the origin of the state? I think that this is in part due to the fact that they were both arch-individualists. In this respect they are, to some extent, products of their own era. Rising individualism is, after all, a characteristic feature of the sixteenth and seventeenth centuries. They were both preoccupied with the independence of man, with man's isolation from his fellow man. Consequently the problem of the origin of political society became magnified. How do such isolated and independent men get together? We who tend on the whole to be much less individualistic and more inclined to assume along with Aristotle that human beings by nature live in society, are not as plagued by this problem of the origins of political orders and states. There is another possible explanation for Hobbes' and Machiavelli's emphasis on the origin of the state. It is in this period that the modern state emerged. In 1500 there could still be some doubt as to whether the decentralized feudal order had passed. In 1650 there could not be. By the middle of the seventeenth century the modern state had come to stay. Such a revolutionary development was naturally a matter of great and persistent concern for thoughtful people. How could this have happened, they asked, what is its explanation? The first efforts to answer these questions were of a philosophical nature, stressing the abstract roots of obligation. Only later, in the generation following Hobbes, did people begin to make historical studies rather than write philosophical treatises on the origins of the political order. Only then did writers begin to trace the development of this extraordinary kind of organization by detailed historical inquiry.

The final issue that I want to deal with is the question of whether it is possible in any precise or detailed sense to label Machiavelli and Hobbes as forerunners of totalitarianism. I would answer this question in the negative. At the present time one of the favorite pastimes, as it has been for the past generation, is tracing the roots of totalitarianism to various hitherto respected forerunners. Nearly everyone has come in for his share of the blame from Marx and Engels to Luther and St. Augustine. Perhaps for politeness sake only, Jesus Christ is omitted from the list. But since Luther and St. Augustine were rather preoccupied with the thought of Christ he is brought in through the back door. In any case there is more to this argument in the case of some writers than of others. Two of whom this is particularly true are Machiavelli and Hobbes. Like the totalitarians they do have this emphasis on power in their writings. This emphasis on power is something that has come under serious scrutiny in our times by the depth psychologists. The authoritarian personality is now a preoccupation with psychoanalysts. It has almost gotten to the point where it is assumed that if one is too keen about power it means that some very dreadful thing happened to you when very tiny. There is nothing you can do about it; your authoritarian bent is irreversible. The emphasis on power in modern psychological studies and in the writings of Machiavelli and Hobbes is shared with totalitarianism. This emphasis, however, is not really the heart of the totalitarian phenomenon of our time in its most specific sense. Emphasis on power is a recurrent theme in the history of political thought and institutions. There is nothing surprising or novel about it. What is almost completely lacking in both Machiavelli and Hobbes are the distinctive characteristics of totalitarianism which include its emphasis on an ideology and connected with this its emphasis on party, the elitist status of which results from an understanding and acceptance of this ideology. There are certain other organizational features of a totalitarian dictatorship like secret police and monopoly of weapons which I leave aside here. These two central features, the ideology and its carrier the party, are the unique and dynamic force that they have become in the twentieth century because this ideology is of a particular kind in a totalitarian movement. It is inspired by a belief on the one hand that the existing society is totally wrong, and totally to be condemned, and on the other hand by the belief that a total reconstruction is possible in terms of the ideology that is expounded. The totalitarian ideology contains both a critique and a program. It can be argued that all ideology performs this dual function, but totalitarian ideology is unique in the totality of both critique and reform. Unlike the Nazi ideology the communist totalitarian ideology is further inspired by a philosophy of history, an eschatological conception of the course of history. I've talked about this earlier in the course so I just remind you of it here. This philosophy of history lends to the organizational claim of the movement a specific force and vigor. It is, so-to-speak, determined by history that the result and outcome of the revolutionary effort will be what the ideology claims. All the activities that must be organized to bring it about are merely helpful assistance to something that is going to happen anyhow.

This entire frame of reference of totalitarian thought is completely alien to Hobbes and Machiavelli. I have just pointed out to you that they were both archindividualists. Machiavelli envisioned an individual hero who could actually reshape a society in his image. No such fancies are found in Marxism. Marx would have considered such notions complete and absurd obscurantism. The individual can do nothing himself to shape history. History is its own law and all one can do is try and understand it. Once it is understood one can help it along. In Hobbes the situation is very similar. In contrast to Machiavelli, his writings bear even less relation to history. Hobbes is ahistorical in the deepest sense. There is no such thing as an eschatological fulfillment for men. This cannot happen. The only thing that can happen is what has always happened. People unite and subject themselves more or less miserably to the kind of rule found all over the globe. There is no sense of perfectionism anywhere in Hobbes. There is no notion that there could be a good society which man could construct. For this reason I would say that Hobbes lacks the pseudo-religious impulse and zeal required of the totalitarian. In this respect it is important to realize that in many ways, particularly in the realm of thought control and uniformity, the Middle Ages, against which both Machiavelli and Hobbes fought so vigorously, were closer to the totalitarianism of the modern era than is the thought of Hobbes and Machiavelli. They had no use for any of the trappings of totalitarianism. I think it quite fair to say that they were both valiant fighters for modern man against medieval collectivism. At the same time, and I hope I brought this out, their thought is marred by their preoccupation with power. Both their strength and their weakness lie in the fact that they articulated the problem of power in a dramatic and challenging way. At the same time, however, by positing power as an absolute they gainsaid the richness, variety and complexity of human existence.

READINGS, SUGGESTED AND REQUIRED

Lectures 9 and 10:

REQUIRED READING:

THOMAS HOBBES, *Leviathan* (Collier): Part I, Chs. 10–16; Part II.
NICCOLO MACHIAVELLI, *The Prince*, tr. Caponigri (Gateway).
JOHN PLAMENATZ, *Man and Society*, Vol. I, Chs. 1, 4 (McGraw-Hill).

SUGGESTIONS FOR FURTHER READING:

Authority, ed. Friedrich, Nomos I (Harvard).
HERBERT BUTTERFIELD, *Statecraft of Machiavelli* (Collier).
FREDERICO CHABOD, *Machiavelli and the Renaissance* (Harvard).
ROBERT FILMER, *Patriarcha*, ed. Laslett. Cf. J. Locke's *First Treatise* (Hofner).
BERTRAND DE JOUVENEL, *On Power* (Beacon).
HENRY S. KARIEL, *In Search of Authority* (The Free Press).
HAROLD LASSWELL, *Politics: Who Gets What, When, and How* (Smith, Peter).
NICCOLO MACHIAVELLI, *Discourses* (Modern Library).
FREDERICK MEINECKE, *Machiavellism* (Praeger).
CHARLES MERRIAM, *Political Power* (Collier).
RAYMOND POLIN, *Politique et Philosophie chez Thomas Hobbes* (Presses Universitaires de France).
YVES SIMON, *Authority* (University of Notre Dame).
LEO STRAUS, *The Political Philosophy of Thomas Hobbes* (University of Chicago Press).
FREDERICK M. WATKINS, *The State as a Concept of Political Science*
MAX WEBER, *The Theory of Social and Economic Organization*, Part III. (The Free Press).

II

Political Equality and the Common Man

THE SENSE FOR EQUALITY as fairness is deeply rooted in men's minds everywhere. That one man should have more of anything desirable than another cannot but seem unfair to the less favored one. This is as true of political power as of anything else. Such a belief in the equality of human beings has in turn been linked to a "belief in the common man," and more particularly in the common man's ability to participate effectively and usefully in the political life of the community, in controlling the government and in evaluating policies. Both beliefs have come under increasingly heavy criticism even while democracy has been spreading. Or perhaps it would be more correct to say, *because* democracy has in this century become more and more universal.

We might start with a general observation on equality found in the work of a most extraordinary writer of our own era. Simone Weil, whose words I am going to cite, was a young member of the French existentialist group. As a Jewess, she was persecuted by the Nazis and ultimately she died of starvation while in hiding.

In her most famous book, *The Need for Roots,* this courageous woman wrote: "Equality is a vital need of the human soul. It consists in a recognition at once public, general, effective and genuinely expressed in institutions and customs, that the same amount of respect and consideration is due to every human being, because this respect is due to the human being as such and is not a matter of degree."

These sentences express a sentiment widely felt in the modern world, a sentiment that at present profoundly agitates the United States as well as other countries. Yet this noble sentiment contradicts basic political experience. While it is easy to claim that this equality of which Simone Weil so eloquently speaks is indivisible and absolute, nevertheless, we all recognize that there can be more or less equality. Indeed, much of our political activity in connection with equality is motivated by this recognition. There is no doubt that it is meaningful to say that the Negro in the United States has more equality today than he did 50 years ago. Perhaps now we realize that Orwell was not so paradoxical. You remember, I am sure, the famous comment of the big pig to the horse in Orwell's *Animal Farm,* "of course everybody is equal, but some are more equal than others." To say that some are more equal than others sounds paradoxical, if not absurd; yet there is clearly such a thing as being more equal than others. It is true that whites in the United States are more equal than Negroes. To be sure, the Negro possesses more equality than he did a while back and hopefully he will possess even more in 20 years than he does now. But it is fair to predict that even in 20 years the American Negro will not be as equal as the whites, nor will Negro and white together be wholly equal. Thus we find a perplexing contrast between this need for an equality which is absolute and the reality of equality which is relative to a great variety of factors and conditions. More especially political equality will always be imperiled by the difference in power possessed by individuals and groups. It is one of the basic laws of politics that no one readily yields powers; he has to be forced to.

The Declaration of Independence states that human beings are

born equal, but most people tend to mock this as merely a nice normative statement which in actuality is absurd, for human beings are not equal. And yet they are claimed to be. Thomas Hobbes, whom we discussed in Lecture X, was probably the first of great political philosophers who specifically sought to give an underpinning to this argument for equality. Hobbes insisted that human beings were by nature equal. It might seem a bit surprising in view of his absolutist propensities, but Hobbes begins chapter 13 of the *Leviathan* with the observation that, "nature has made men so equal in the faculties of body and mind as that though there be found one man sometimes manifestly stronger in body or of quicker mind than another, yet when all is reckoned together the difference between man and man is not so considerable as that one man can thereupon claim to himself any benefit to which another may not pretend as well as he." This is an existential statement which asserts that men are, all things considered, pretty much alike. There may be some differences but these differences are not very considerable and certainly not considerable enough to constitute a ground for any just claims of superiority. This is probably the first time that equality has been argued in existential terms. Hobbes is not claiming that human beings ought to be equal, or that they ought to be equal before the law. His claim is that men are in fact equal. Hobbes' insistence upon the existential equality of human beings is due to his concern with power, yet it is a position radically at variance with political experience.

Men have always been politically unequal. Indeed, it may be doubted that "political equality" in a strict meaning makes sense. Why then could it become one of the great battle cries of political oratory? What is the political situation in which the demand for political equality arises? To put it another way: although it is a common observation that men are treated differently and behave differently in all known political communities, the demand is made that they should all be treated equally and that they shall all act, *as if* they were equals. As against such demands, the actual political *in*equality is easy to understand. It is usually based upon what the

community believes to be qualities or virtues required for various kinds of political tasks.

In recent decades a great effort to achieve equality has been made by the underprivileged groups in this country and throughout the world. But at the same time there has been a steady erosion of the radical egalitarianism of the past. The faith in equality which played so large a role in American intellectual and social history is today hardly defended in its pure and radical form. It might be worthwhile to restate this pure and radical image of equality which has been such a force since the days of Rousseau. Such a view would have it that all social inequalities are unnecessary. It was a view developed as a protest against the privileges of an aristocracy which derived from the feudal age. This protest had its religious roots in, indeed was a secularized version of, man's creaturely insignificance before a lofty deity. "We are all miserable sinners," men had said for many ages. Now they said: "We are all worthy men." In the famous words of a soldier in Cromwell's army: "the poorest he that is in England hath a life to live as the greatest he." (Thomas Rainsboro in the Army Debates at Putney.) Any inequality of treatment, especially in politics, is unjustifiable and ought to be eliminated. Very few people are really prepared to take this position today. Reverting to views of the time before Rousseau, various kinds of inequalities have come to be recognized as inevitable and even to be considered justifiable. Hence in our age the goal of elimination of inequality has been abandoned and men differentiate between the kinds of inequality that can and ought to be eliminated.

But let me recall that egalitarian notion of a hundred years ago primarily concerning political equality rather than equality in general, the central position of the political egalitarian Mill, stated in his *Representative Government*. "There is no difficulty in showing," wrote Mill, "that the ideally best form of government is that in which the sovereign or supreme controlling power is vested in the last resort in the entire aggregate of the community, every citizen not only having a voice in the exercise of that sovereignty, but being at least occasionally called upon to take an active part in the government by the personal discharge of some public function, local or general." This statement of Mill puts well if a bit pompously the prevailing view in England, America, and other English-speaking countries. Political equality for these countries tends to be seen as universal popular government. Yet I think we could hardly agree with Mill today in his claim that there was no difficulty in showing that the ideally best form of government is the one in which sovereignty is vested in the entire aggregate of the community. We may still believe this to be the case, but whether we do or not, few of us would be inclined to deceive ourselves into thinking that there was *no difficulty* in showing that one should prefer popular sovereignty in terms of effective operation. It has ceased to be considered self-evident.

What is the reason for this change since Mill wrote *Representative Government?* It is to some extent a result of the concrete and practical experience of the communities in which some approximation of this democratic ideal has been attempted. It is also a result of a considerable amount of writing which considers what actually occurs to human beings when placed in a democratic and egalitarian condition. Inquiries into mass psychology have been producing disquieting results. They tend to render problematic what is at the bottom of this belief in the intrinsic desirability of the active participation of all men in their government, namely what I would call the rationalist image of men. This image you can see quite clearly and explicitly in a key writer of the American Revolution, Thomas Paine. To epitomize what Thomas Paine said in many different ways in his several writings, one might put it thus: Give the simple mind of the ordinary man the facts and he will see the rational and reasonable way to act. Having perceived this way, he will follow it." Today, unfortunately, we are beset with doubts about each one of the component elements of this proposition. We would start by saying that it is not clear what the facts are. What are the facts that one should give to the simple mind of the ordinary man? Men in official positions, especially in foreign offices, usually are convinced that the public does not and cannot know the facts upon which the policy of the government is based. At the same time they are reluctant to state what these facts are; journalists and the public complain that they are not given the facts, or that the government is overlooking other important facts. This, then, is the first of our difficulties. There is much uncertainty about what the facts are which one ought to furnish the simple mind of the ordinary man. The second area of doubt surrounds Paine's claim that the ordinary man will see the rational and the reasonable way to act. Common experience has shown that not only the simple mind of the ordinary man, but also the highly sophisticated mind of the academic man will not necessarily see the reasonable and rational way to act. Often what man sees is related to his particular prejudices, his particular interests, and so forth and so on. But even if it should occasionally happen that the common man does see the reasonable and rational way to act, there are further doubts concerning Paine's third point that, having perceived the rational course, man will follow it. There are altogether too numerous instances in which people fully aware of the reasonable and rational way do not follow it. Passions and other human frailties get in the way.

In short, if you examine any concrete political situation which confronts you or your friends at the present time, you will see that every one of these three implicit premises of the rationalist image upon which Paine and others built their appeal is subject to very serious doubt. What we are really confronted with here is a construct, a model of a rational political man which corresponds to the model of the rational economic man of classical economics. Today, however, even fewer believe in the reality of the rational political man than in the reality of the economic man.

What accounts for this radical reappraisal of the nature of political man and the downgrading of his powers of reason and hence of his ability for self-government? Two thinkers are particularly important in this connection because they were greatly concerned with the disclosure of the hidden recesses of human motivation. One, of course, is Karl Marx with whom we started these lectures, and the other is Sigmund Freud with whom we might end if some students of politics had their way. I myself believe, as I said to you a little earlier, that nobody today, whether or not he reads Marx or Freud, can escape the intellectual impact of these two giants of the nineteenth and early twentieth century. Their analysis was so trenchant and so compelling that they have become part and parcel of all inquiry and discourse. Nobody would today think of talking about politics or history without taking the economic determinant into account. Nobody today writes a book, a biography, or a novel without alluding to the sub-conscious, the factors not recognized by the individual which have a decided influence in shaping his life and his behavior. After the writings of Marx and Freud it has become virtually impossible for a thoughtful person in the mid-twentieth century to accept the rationalist image prevailing in the early nineteenth century. The factual data that have been accumulated, not only in politics but in the analysis of society and man, make these propositions untenable. With the exposure of non-rational man has come the questioning of popular sovereignty, since at its center stood a belief in the rational political man.

What has grown from all this is, of course, the familiar anti-rationalist challenge that has filled this century. Let us further illustrate this trend with Nietzsche, who wrote between Marx and Freud and who, while contributing his share to this basic reappraisal of man, has also ably articulated the discontent and uncertainty over how to proceed once this reappraisal has destroyed one of the basic assumptions on which democracy is built, namely that concerning equality. Like many today, Nietzsche revolted against the mass man. At the beginning of *Thus Spake Zarathustra,* Zarathustra deals with the "last" man in bitter, if poetic words. " 'What is love, what is creation, what is longing, what is a star?' asks the last man and blinks. The earth has become small and upon it hops the last man who belittles anything and everything. His species is ineradicable like the earth flea. . . . No shepherd and one flock. Each wants the same, each is the same. He who feels differently enters the insane asylum of his own accord. . . . A little lust for the day and a little lust for the night, but one honors good health. 'We have invented happiness,' say the last men and blink."

Here you have one of the most poignant early expressions of the revulsion felt by many men against the modern mass man. One readily recognizes in this horrid portrayal a substantial percentage of our contemporaries even if we do not yet recognize ourselves and occasionally we may manage to do even that. Nietzsche contrasts mass man, this earth-flea, this sanitary average man, with the superman. The superman is particularly described in his *Will to Power*. Feeling that there is approaching the great task and question of how the globe as a whole is to be administered, he calls for "a certain strong kind of man of highest spirit and will to power." This new kind of man does not yet exist. They will be "the lords of the earth; Englishmen, Americans, Russians." He explicitly excluded the Germans because they seemed to him tedious pedants who did not have the kind of spirit needed to be supermen. For the superman is not merely a politician or a warrior, or even a statesman. No, Nietzsche adopts the Platonic position. The super superman is the philosopher, seen as legislator, exactly as in the Platonic academy. After then describing the extraordinary qualities such wise guardians ruling the world must possess, Nietzsche concludes that this philosopher-king can only come into being as the member of a ruling class as its highest spiritual incarnation.

Nietzsche's ideas were the epitome of a kind of thinking which gradually spread in twentieth-century Europe, but not only in Europe. For example, in his *Notes on Democracy*, Mencken, a great admirer of Nietzsche, rejected in sardonic, indeed carbolic terms, the make-believe of American society after the first World War. Here we see the anti-democratic potential inherent in this disillusionment with the picture of rational man.

We are, then, confronted by rising discontent with a political doctrine that rests upon assumptions which have largely been eroded. Out of this loss of belief in the common man are spawned the ideas of fascism, national socialism, and totalitarian communism. This has been a wide-spread reaction of many intellectuals, but it seems to some, and I am very strongly of this opinion my-self, that perhaps a restatement of the egalitarian and democratic position can be undertaken in terms of a different image of man.

A possible approach to this restatement may be found in the writings of Thorstein Veblen. He was deeply immersed in the American tradition and while a sharp critic of American society, he insisted upon a retention of the belief in the common man. At one point in his analysis of the common man Veblen made a point quite significant in light of the critique found in the writings of men such as Nietzsche, Marx, and Freud. Veblen wrote: "The common man is constantly and increasingly exposed to the risk of becoming an undesirable citizen in the eyes of the votaries of law and order." In this statement there is already discernible something in the way of a radical differentiation between the common man and the mass man. Obviously he is not talking of the mass man, or the last man; he means someone else. He is describing what would perhaps be more properly called the communal man, rather than the common man. I think that on the basis of this distinction there exists the possibility of a radical reassessment of the old position which would make it both impervious to the objections that have arisen against it and more realistic in terms of the opera-tions of democratic political orders.

Some of the extreme claims of writers like Paine were due to the fact that they were writing against a traditional and thorough-going elitism. He proceeded as did many others, like Benjamin Franklin, to make claims for the common man as unrealistic as the elite position had claimed for the elite. It is possible to turn Paine's argument around by asking: is this kind of claim true with reference to the elite? In other words rather than assert the superi-ority of the common man, one might assert the non-superiority of the alleged elite man.

Now if you proceed on the assumption which I think the premises I have been developing for you make inescapable, namely that the rationalist image of man is fraudulent, I think you come to four counter-propositions which realistically assess the common man and the sphere for the participation of equals in the political order. First, the common man is fallible, but so are all men; second, we need the collective judgments of the common man and not his individual judgments; third, in dealing with political equality we are looking for judgments on common problems, and not on problems involving highly discriminating judgment. Finally, character and the steady appreciation of the role of values and beliefs, that is to say the convictional core of human behavior, are more important than intellect for the resolution of political problems. I could elaborate on this for a good deal more time than we have here, but let me make just a few comments on these four propositions. Rather than say that the common man is infallible, one says the common man is fallible because all men are fallible. In politics one deals with contingent situations in which fallibility cannot be avoided. The belief, first found among elitists and then among democrats, that you could find human beings who were always right is mere pretense and conceit. No will of any kind is always right, whether it be the general will of Rousseau or a will derived from the divine right of an absolute monarch like Louis XIV. All men are sometimes wrong. This leads immediately to the second proposition: that we are concerned with collective judgments and not individual judgments. The traditional elitist argument is one which says that I, Professor Friedrich, am probably better able to form a judgment on Vietnam than my taxi driver. But this traditional position misses the point. In the organized process of political argumentation the question is not whether the position of one particular man is better than that of another particular man. Such positions merely organize discussion and debate and consequently organize the development of collective judgments on the issues at hand. Even Aristotle, who was rather an elitist, made it quite clear in the *Politics* that he thought the collective judgment of many people tended to be superior in matters involving contingencies, to the judgment of an individual man, no matter how clever he might be. This view was taken over and used again by Machiavelli in his defense of republican government. But even this would not really rescue us if it were not for the fact that the many problems that have to be solved in the political context are common problems. There is one exception to this and it is a very bothersome one, foreign policy. I will not go into that here at length. Briefly, my own view is that democracy is not fully compatible with foreign policy and therefore seeks to eliminate foreign policy either by isolation or by world-wide organization; in either case foreign policy disappears. But, leaving foreign policy aside, the kind of problems that have to be solved in the political context are common problems. In other words they are not the kind of problems which necessitate a discriminating judgment as is the case in judging the beauty of works of art, or the sanctity of the conduct of religious persons. Political problems do not even involve the kind of discrimination in taste which enables one to say "this wine is superior to that wine." Political judgments are judgments on common problems that touch a large number of people. These large numbers of people are capable of forming an effective collective judgment because a great deal of this judgment turns on the values, interests and beliefs prevalent in a particular community. This brings me to the fourth point, that of the comparative importance of character as contrasted with intellect and the importance of values. In politics, particularly under contemporary conditions, continuity or consistency is extremely important. This consistency is possible only when firmly anchored in the prevalent values, interests and beliefs of the political community for which the policy decisions have to be developed. Such consistency is closely linked to loyalty and dependability. The man of agile mind is too readily able to invent rationalizations for departing from values, norms and beliefs which the community cherishes. It is an aspect of politics which the intellectual is prone to overlook. The German philosopher Kant has put this notion most effectively, though he did so primarily in the moral rather than the political perspective. In his *Metaphysical Foundations of Morals* he argues that we do not need science and philosophy to know what we should do to be honest and good and even wise and virtuous. Very much in contrast to Plato and Nietzsche, he praised common sense, like Locke and Paine. In the practical sphere, he thought "the power of judgment of common sense shows itself to particular advantage." Disparaging all subtle arguments, he claims that when it comes to "hitting the mark" in practical affairs "a common man is most sure of doing so." Therefore, he believes that it would be wiser "to acquiesce in the judgment of common reason." This common reason gives men their "character," their steadfastness in maintaining what is right. (My selections, p. 152) Kant's thought here is an elaboration of the view of the great Chinese philosopher, Confucius, who said that "character is the backbone of human nature and music is the flowering of character." In other words, great creative achievements are by no means only or primarily intellectual achievements; they are achievements whose firmness consists in being grounded in values and beliefs that are shared by the community.

Against this background I would like to project two important distinctions which draw this analysis to a conclusion. Let me remind you first, however, that by this restating of the position of the common man we also escape from a difficulty which is presented by the persistent anti-intellectualism found in the American democratic tradition. Richard Hofstadter, in his history of anti-intellectualism in American life, reviews the persistency of this strand in American culture. This anti-intellectualist position, connected with the egalitarianism prevalent in American life, is a perfectly understandable reaction once you see the limits of the rational intellect and no longer engage in the rationalist pride. One may then discern the true possibilities of human beings placed into positions of ever greater equality.

Now let us turn to the two important general points which need to be made here to conclude our discussion of equality. One is that we must distinguish between general and legal equality. The traditional formula is "equality before the law." A good many people though dubious about other kinds of equality accept equality before the law. Yet, equality before the law is curious, for it invariably means some kind of classification. For example, equality before the income tax law does not mean that everyone pays the same income tax. On the contrary it means that everyone pays a different income tax, depending upon his income. This same principle can be traced through all the different spheres of law. One could almost go so far as to say that unless there is a need for classification, i.e., differentiation, there is no need for law. Law arises as a result of the need to spell out what is to be understood by equality before the law in any particular legal context. Originally, of course, equality before the law was a formula to be used against the privileges of a special class. Originally it meant that no person could come into a court and claim that he must be treated differently because he was a count or because he had a great deal of money or some other kind of specific difference. There are still times and places where this sort of thing occurs but it is generally thought to be unjust and a violation of legal equality, that is to say equality before the law.

The second general point to be made is the distinction between political equality and legal equality. Our central concern is with political equality. What is to be understood by political equality? Basically, I think, political equality must be understood as the equal opportunity to participate in the acquisition and experience of governmental power, in short, participation in government. No particular quality is admitted as providing a satisfactory index for the capacity to govern. This is, you might say, the exciting part of the doctrine of political equality. In the past and indeed, in many societies to this day, the contrary opinion is held, which would see either wealth, noble descent, great intellectual ability, or something else of that sort as an indicator of the capacity to govern. Democratic equality is based on the notion that this is untrue, that there is no such indicator. And because there is no such indicator, the only way one can find the politically talented person is to open the political arena to the participation of all. "Give all men and women an equal opportunity to govern," runs the legend. By the use made of this opportunity there will emerge those with a particular capacity for government. This is the crucial issue involved in the idea of political equality. Now you might come back and ask does such political equality ever exist, even if refined and defined as the opportunity to participate in the acquisition of power. The answer of course is that in the strict sense

it does not. In the United States wealth makes a substantial difference and hence limits the equality of opportunity. In the U. S. S. R.
membership in the party hierarchy makes a substantial difference
in one's ability to participate in government. It is rather interesting in this score to recall a saying of Lenin's when challenged in
1919 with the query, whether this is supposed to be equality. He
answered: "Any demand for equality that goes beyond the demand
for the abolition of classes is a stupid and absurd prejudice."
What does this mean? It meant that the revolution sought only to
achieve the disappearance of privileged, and more especially ruling
classes. Political equality in the sense of opportunity for participation was not necessarily involved. Even so, I think one has to
conclude that at present both constitutionalist and totalitarian
systems provide for more political equality than did past regimes.
This progress is a product of the nearly universal *dis*belief in
manifest innate qualities of which I have spoken.

The increase in political equality is an ongoing process. At this
very moment we in the United States are going through an agoniz-
ing process of greatly extending political equality in the sense of
expanding the opportunity for political participation. Once you
reassess the position of the common man and equality and no
longer allow yourself to be misled by the rationalist model, you
are in a much better position. You are no longer claiming what
cannot really be claimed today. Consequently, you can, for example, argue that it is desirable to find out whether there is not
among our colored population some remarkable political talent.
I have a very strong suspicion that this discovery will be made
because where Negroes have turned up in politics they have displayed a substantial political capacity.

Once one reassesses his views on equality, along the lines I
have suggested today, one is in a much better position to maintain
the kind of limited but at the same time stouter belief in the
future of constitutional democracy which I for one cherish.

12

Equality in Rousseau and Kant

N to one in the history of political thought is more
strongly identified with the problem of equality and the
belief in the common man than Jean Jacques Rousseau.
He strikes us as a bit antiquated today, because he wrote at a time
when inequalities were common and still widely accepted as the
natural condition of man and the political order. Since then, a
considerable measure of doubt has sprung up about whether it is
"natural" for men to be unequal in income and life's amenities and
opportunities, including more especially the participation in politics. Not only the American Declaration of Independence and its
ringing phrases, but the French Revolution and the rise of democracy all over the world have produced such a change in outlook that anyone arguing for inequality of any sort, but more
particularly political inequality, finds himself with the burden of
proof. He has to show why such inequality may be in the public
interest, e.g., why judges should be appointed on account of their
legal training and skilled wisdom, rather than *elected* like other
high officials.

Yet, although fairly radical in his egalitarianism, Rousseau does
not greatly elaborate his thought on equality. In the *Discourse*

(about which something more in a moment) he is concerned with *in*equality, and in the *Social Contract,* his major political work, he devotes only part of a chapter on legislation to it (Bk. II, ch. XI). In this brief analysis, he clearly speaks of *political* equality and he puts the case rather moderately. He very sanely remarks that one should not mean by it that "the degrees of power and riches are absolutely identical for everybody." What he considers essential is that in the first place power ought not to be so great that its possessor can engage in lawless violence. And what he in the second place makes a standard for political equality is that power be exercised only "by virtue of rank and law." Finally, Rousseau adds that as far as wealth is unequal, it ought never to be so great that its possessor could buy another citizen, and no one so poor that he would sell himself. In this latter thought the familiar plea of Aristotle for a broad middle class is implied, and Rousseau admits as much in a footnote. These rather modestly egalitarian views are nonetheless controversial. Rousseau reminds the reader that "such equality is an unpractical ideal," according to many. Rousseau admits that "abuse is inevitable," but precisely for that reason "legislation should always tend to its [equality's] maintenance." Even so, Rousseau believes that laws should be "in agreement with the natural relations" and warns against trying to use them against nature; for if they are so used, they will "insensibly lose their influence" until eventually the state is destroyed or changed and "nature has resumed her invincible sway." It would be too easy to argue that Rousseau contradicts himself. It is Rousseau's true opinion that equality is "natural," as are liberty and war, and that therefore the laws are directed to maintaining such equality against the corrupting influence of power-hungry individuals.

Rousseau's failure to elaborate his argument is no doubt due to the fact that by the mid-eighteenth century despite the practice of inequality the *belief* in human equality had become very much a matter of course. The French Enlightenment, though basically inclined toward intellectual elitism, had by its animosity toward aristocratic privilege prepared the way. Yet it was Rousseau who really provided the breakthrough. We have eloquent testimony for that by none other than the great philosopher and admirer of Rousseau, Immanuel Kant. After describing himself as "by nature a seeker after truth" and recalling that there was a time when he believed that thought and knowledge alone "constitute the honor of mankind" he confesses that he "despised the common man who knows nothing." So far, Kant speaks as the typical representative of the Enlightenment and its intellectual snobbery. But then he states: "Rousseau set me right. This blind prejudice vanished. I learned to respect human nature." These statements bear clear evidence to Rousseau's egalitarian impact. Even so, Rousseau does not particularly elaborate upon equality. What he does argue is a question put at the start of the *Social Contract:* "Man is born free; and everywhere he is in chains." Why? He does not feel that he can explain how this came about, but he does believe he can suggest what could make it legitimate. In other words, what he wishes to say by this dramatic exclamation is: how can it be explained that there is so much inequality in the treatment of men, when by nature they are born equal? It is the central theme of one of the works of Rousseau you are asked to read, the *Discourse on the Origin of Inequality*. The problem in this essay is that of inequality rather than equality. The answer which he gave was that inequality was due to the rise of civilization. Originally, men were living a simple life which let them all be roughly equal. Then, as they progressed toward more and more complicated relationships, *amour propre* or self-esteem transformed these easy-going savages into striving competitive but increasingly civilized men. Yet, he does not want to have this understood as "history." Rather, it is what we nowadays call a "model" and a poetic model at that. At the outset he asks the reader "to lay facts aside," because in his view the question is a theoretical one. The inquiry he has undertaken, Rousseau tells us, "must not be considered as [containing] historical truths, but only mere conditional and hypothetical reasonings." Their purpose is to "explain the nature of things" and he even compares his procedure to that of the physicist when he makes "hypotheses respecting the formation of the world." Rousseau, then, means by origin the "reason" or "explanation" of inequality.

Before we go more deeply into all the implications of this basic argument of Rousseau, let me first say a word or two about Rousseau the man and the writer. His dates, 1712–1778, place him squarely in the eighteenth century. He was not French, although he is often considered French because he wrote in French. He was in fact born in Geneva, and through his life of restless wandering he became a cosmopolitan European. Still, he remained passionately attached to Switzerland and to his native Geneva in spite of the fact that the canton of Geneva did not treat him very well. Some of his radical and democratic propensities probably derived from the age-long democratic traditions of the small rural cantons in Switzerland from which the Swiss confederacy had sprung in the Middle Ages. These original cantons, Schwyz, Uri and Unterwalden, have to this day remained so small that the peasants who constitute most of the population still gather together in an annual popular assembly, somewhat like our New England town meetings.

The relation of Rousseau to France was something in the way of a spiritual affinity. Rousseau himself has dramatically described this in his *Confessions*. *The Confessions*, by the way, is a most remarkable review of Rousseau's life. It is an autobiography of extraordinary frankness if not necessarily of comparable reliability. The franker we become about ourselves the more apt we are to be wrong, because the more apt we are to express a purely subjective view which few others are inclined to share. This is very true of Rousseau's *Confessions*, in a way the most remarkable document of exhibitionism which exists in European letters. Rousseau alludes, of course, to St. Augustine's famous work. But far from "confessing" to a state of sin, he proclaims the dignity of his nature and undertakes to explain, if not to justify, all his actions. In any case, as I said, Rousseau writes in these *Confessions* of his love for the French. He describes himself in Paris as having "played the part of the enemy of tyrants and the proud republican." "I felt," he writes, "in spite of myself a secret predilection for this very nation I found servile and for the government which I pretended to condemn." Further on he says again, "I loved them in spite of myself, in spite of their ill-treatment of me." Elsewhere he describes his interest in French letters and arts as being finally "converted into a blind infatuation which nothing has been able to overcome." These few sentences show you that Rousseau looked upon France and the French as an outsider would, as someone profoundly attached to its people and culture; but not one of them.

I would like to raise at this point a question which in a sense is biographical. Was Rousseau, as he is so often described, the apostle of the French Revolution? He certainly has been so considered by many people over the years. And to this day some of the positions he developed have been slogans in the armory of democratic revolutionaries all over the world. And yet, was that really his own intention? I raise this question partly because in recent years the pendulum has swung the other way and Rousseau has been described as a conservative. There is no doubt that Rousseau had a profound hatred for revolution. There is in fact one passage in the *Confessions* in which he describes his attitude toward revolution by recounting a particular experience he had had as a young man when a little rebellion broke out in Geneva. After a dramatic description of the crowds in the streets, he informs the reader that this experience filled him with a lasting horror of revolution. Rousseau, then, was not like Locke a defender of revolution. This, of course, does not necessarily exclude the possibility of Rousseau's being an inspiration for the French revolutionaries. It is well worth remembering, however, because it contrasts Rousseau with Locke on the one hand and Marx on the other, both of whom were intimately linked to great revolutions, and both of whom positively accepted revolution. On the other hand one cannot hide the fact that the Jacobins, who were the radicals of the French Revolution, virtually deified Rousseau. Their little Jacobin clubs were bare and puritanical in appearance, yet usually they contained a picture of Rousseau alongside a statue of the goddess of reason. The fact that Rousseau had struggled to overcome the Enlightenment's preoccupation with reason and rationality did not prevent the Jacobin clubs from celebrating the two together. Some have said that the revolutionaries misunderstood Rousseau. This is particularly a favored argument with academic pedants who consider themselves wise. They often, hundreds of years later, tell a startled world that the contemporaries did not understand the issues of their day and that a particular thinker meant something quite different than what his contemporaries thought he had in mind. Such interpreters have usually read their book by the proverbial candlelight, detached, uninvolved and uncommitted. Such a reading leads one to interpret passages differently than if one had read a book with the passions and preoccupations of the author and his contemporaries. I myself am inclined to think that we have to give our central attention as students of politics to how the contemporary understood a given writing because that is the form in which it worked. My contention would thus be that one of the things which particularly aroused the enthusiasm and commitment of French revolutionaries was Rousseau's belief in and concern with equality, his belief in equality and his concern over inequality. The revolutionaries were radical egalitarians opposing a hierarchical society based on belief in an elite. Some of the bitter sentiments Rousseau felt for the philosophers, like Voltaire, were aroused by their association with the ideas of enlightened despotism. He opposed their belief that the philosophers should rule together with crowned monarchs, autocrats like Frederick II of Prussia, Catherine of Russia, and Joseph of Austria, all three of whom bear the epithet "great" in the history books. Rousseau opposed the philosopher's belief that if only the despot grasped the principles expounded by men like Voltaire he would be able to create a good society. Against this type of intellectualist elitism Rousseau was profoundly aroused and determined to overcome it, like the revolutionaries who followed him.

This leads to another question which has agitated our own time rather than the preceding generation. Was Rousseau a totalitarian? Can he be understood as providing the seedbed of totalitarianism?

Such an interpretation would not necessarily be in conflict with his egalitarian views, for totalitarian ideologies are propagating equality. Hence this thesis, quite popular in some quarters, has been learnedly expounded in a well-known and very interesting book, *Totalitarian Democracy,* written by Professor Talmon of the Hebrew University in Jerusalem. Talmon interprets Rousseau as a kind of progenitor of the totalitarian philosophy. He suggests that Rousseau's thinking leads straight to the Terror of the Revolution with all its tyrannical autocracy. Now, it is true that there are certain formulas in Rousseau that have some link with the radical collectivism of the totalitarians of our time. In this respect people have dwelt especially upon the assertion in the *Social Contract* that people may indeed be "forced to be free." Forced to be free is generally seen as characteristic of the thinking of communist totalitarians who, in the tradition of Marxian philosophy of history, would interpret freedom as the "flowering of necessity." According to the Marxian materialist interpretation, when a communist leader forces people to go along with the predicted course of history, he is forcing them to be free, forcing them to participate in the flowering of necessity. Rousseau's statement, in contrast, has nothing to do with historical eschatologies; it has nothing to do with any type of necessity of that sort. The forcing to be free which Rousseau talks about is, as a matter of fact, a forcing to be free familiar to all of us. It is nothing more than what anyone in the United States or in any constitutional democracy would maintain, namely that freedom is freedom through and under law, that when you are speaking of freedom in a democratic society you do not mean lawless license, you mean behavior in accordance with laws adopted by the majority. This is what Rousseau means when talking of forcing men to be free. It is a constitutionalist rather than a totalitarian conception.

There is another aspect of Rousseau's thought to which I now turn, which is intimately related to his egalitarianism and which may be a more effective argument against those who would consider him a totalitarian. Rousseau's notion of the equality of man is based upon his rejection of inequality. In other words it is really a negative notion. It is a notion which can be stated explicitly as the normative proposition that there shall not be any privileges. In *The Essay on the Origin of Inequality* Rousseau argues that inequality arising in the course of the progress of civilization more particularly results from the institution of property. There is a famous statement from that essay to which I would like to draw your attention. It is a very vivid and concrete proposition. "The first man who having enclosed a piece of ground bethought himself of saying 'this is mine' and found people simple enough to believe him was the real founder of civil society." At that very moment men become different and distinct from each other; they become unequal. The central problem Rousseau wrestles with in his political thinking is finding a way to enable man to overcome this inequality and all the various inequalities through a more satisfactory organization of society.

It is not true, although it is often alleged, that Rousseau saw the state of nature as idyllic because in it people were equal. A recent writer has put it rather neatly in summing up the true position of Rousseau. "Man, then, is a lazy beast, enjoying the sentiment of his own existence, concerned with his preservation and pitying the sufferings of his fellow creatures, free and perfectible." This is the "noble savage" whose image so enchanted the fine ladies at the Court of Versailles in their brocades. It is, to be sure, not an unpleasant state, but it is far from idyllic. It is something which has great potentialities for the future but it requires a great deal in order to become a really satisfactory state.

In the course of his description of the development of society, Rousseau introduces a distinction which is of great importance to his thought and which has given rise to a great deal of controversy. The distinction is in the area which you would expect from a French writer, a distinction in the area of *"amour."* In the state of nature man lives by an *amour de soi* which is most nearly translated into English as G. D. H. Cole does, as self-respect. Literally it means love of oneself in the sense of an appreciation of the self. Contact with other men corrupts this self-respect and turns it into self-esteem. This *amour propre* one might render more broadly as self-love, a selfish concern for oneself and one's superiority to others. The purpose of constructing the good society is to restrain the *amour propre* and provide an opportunity for a redevelopment of *amour de soi,* of our self-respect. Natural man cannot accomplish this alone. We cannot solve our social problems by returning to a state of nature; we can only solve them by building a social order which makes morality secure. Morality presupposes freedom, because only the free man is responsible. Therefore the theme of *The Social Contract* is in a sense freedom. But its celebrated opening sentences (already cited) show that Rousseau does not think of it as dedicated to freedom, but rather to the problem of legitimacy. He himself gave the work the subtitle: *principes de droit politique,* usually translated: principles of political right. The basic political right is that of "legitimizing" political rule. A rule is legitimate, when those who are ruled believe that their rulers have a right to rule them. Clearly, then, there is a basic political equality involved, a minimum equality, we might say, if we recall Rousseau's readiness to accept considerable inequalities of power as well as riches, as I pointed out at the start of this lecture. Every man must be engaged and committed to the system of rule he is subject to, Rousseau means to say.

It is therefore part of the central theme of *The Social Contract* to consider how we can balance self-interest and duty. Rousseau develops his answer in terms of what constitutes legitimacy. It is a tightly woven argument. Rousseau is often blamed for being erratic and contradictory. I myself, however, am, every time I re-read Rousseau, impressed by the extraordinary sweep of his logical coherence. There is something quite bewitching in the way Rousseau builds up his argument step-by-step. There may be some minor logical inconsistencies, but there always are in great writers. On the whole his argument strikes me as remarkably persuasive. In the famous chapter entitled "The Social Contract" you find his central argument. "Our problem is to find a form of association which will defend and protect with the whole common force the person and goods of each associate, and in which each, while uniting himself with all, may still obey himself alone and remain as free as before." One can clearly see from this citation Rousseau's concern with each and hence his emphasis on the equality of the citizen. All must find a satisfactory sphere for their activities in a social order. On the next page he describes the form of association which will accomplish this difficult task. The passage is actually italicized to make unmistakable the importance of this particular point. "If, then, we discard from the Social Compact what is not of its essence we shall find that it reduces itself to the following terms. Each of us puts his person and all his power in common under the supreme direction of the general will. And in our corporate capacity we receive each member as an indivisible part of the whole." What Rousseau is saying is that the self which enters into this new kind of social contract remains indestructible. Now how does this version of the Compact differ from that of Hobbes whom we studied last time and whom you have been reading? Hobbes also thought of a contract as a way of human beings to enter into the obligations which society calls for. But whom do they subject themselves to? The answer to this question marks the vital difference between Hobbes and Rousseau. In Hobbes all the men entering the contract agree with each other to subject themselves to a sovereign who is envisaged as a ruler over them. It may be one man or it may be several, but there is an absolute ruler over the contractants. In Rousseau the citizens subject themselves to what Rousseau calls the "general will."

With this phrase we come to what is at the same time the most striking and the most controversial part of Rousseau's political philosophy. It can only be understood when seen as recognition of equality. Rousseau makes it quite clear that this general will, this *volonté génerale,* is not the will of all in the sense of adding the will of A plus B plus C plus D plus E plus F. Yet it *is* the will of all in the sense that we must consider it as springing from the willing of the entirety of the citizens. But when? Not when men consider their own self-interest, but only when they consider the public interest, the interest of all. The general will is the kind of choice that would result if each one would ask himself "how should the majority act in order to benefit the community?" It can never be found when people ask themselves "how should the majority act in order to benefit myself?" To explain this further Rousseau coined such extraordinary formulations that they have plagued political analysts ever since. One of these is his claim that the general will is always right but that the people whom we consult in order to find out what the general will is might well deceive themselves. The general will in other words is posited as something that is there if only one can find it. The argument is that in the really good community, which is small enough to allow everyone to consult with everyone else, you can find the general will by consulting all. Rousseau holds that in such a general debate, people would gradually be brought around to considering the needs of all, that is the needs of the community rather than their individual needs. If you happen to be a New Englander and have participated in a town meeting you know that this is often what happens when men get together in such a meeting. The notion is that the whole town talking with each other under the guidance of a moderator skilled in eliminating disturbing elements will eventually arrive at the right decision. The general will may thus be found, discovered and expressed in the majority's vote and executed by the select-men. I purposely mention this tradition to show how Rousseau's thinking is quite close to some basic American traditions.

A question which has often been raised is whether the general will is rational. I think the answer is that it depends a great deal, as it always does in arguments about rationality, on how one understands reason. I think that in the intention of Rousseau, it is rational. It is that which reason commands when men have reasonably explored what is relevant to the situation. However, what is relevant to the situation is not merely given material facts and the abstract rationality of their handling but also human emotions. What is relevant to the situation is what people really believe in, what people really value, and what people are really concerned about. One is confronted here with a doctrine which Rousseau brings forward in all his works. We can illustrate it with a sentence from *The Discourse on the Origin of Inequality*. Pushing aside all the scholarly books on the law of nature which he had been reviewing, he wrote: "I think I can perceive in the human soul two principles prior to reason, one of them deeply interesting us in our own welfare and preservation, and the other exciting a natural repugnance at seeing any other sensible being, and particularly any of our own species, suffer pain and death." There are thus two things that Rousseau explicitly says are beyond reason. Our own welfare and preservation are beyond reason and so is compassion. Out of these two basic constituents of the human soul, every human soul, the general will emerges. The general will, in other words, is something that is meta-rational although it is arrived at by reasoning about these meta-rationalities, these values, interests and beliefs.

But clearly all this reasoning applies only to the small community. Rousseau is himself quite explicit on the point. Indeed, at one stage in his argument he even proclaims that "so perfect a government is not for men." Only a people of gods would and could be democratic in Rousseau's view. For large states, autocracy must be accepted. Does this mean that the general will is completely obliterated? No, answers Rousseau; for a good autocrat will try to discover and act according to the general will. There are in Rousseau, traces of authoritarian sentiment. What he has to say about the legislator, the "legislateur," would suggest that he does not exclude the possibility that under certain conditions it might be better to consult a single individual, or perhaps some elite collection of individuals, on what constitutes the general will. Rousseau's views on dictatorship also bear authoritarian overtones. He did not believe that a large country like the United States could be a democracy. Such a country would have to be governed by an autocrat. From the letters of the Russian Empress, Catherine the Great, we know that she appreciated Rousseau because he recognized the necessity for autocracy in large states and that is all she cared about. The Swiss could have their democracy in their little mountain country, but a great Empress was needed to rule all Russia. Alongside his prescription of autocracy for large states,

Rousseau indicated that for a medium-sized country, aristocracy was the right form of government. In both cases the reason is the difficulty of discovering the general will if the number of people becomes so large that they cannot consult with each other and can no longer debate and argue and bring each other to a recognition of what the general will might be. Under such conditions it is better to have some individual or small group express the general will. The argument, advanced by those who see Rousseau as the precursor of totalitarianism, is that this notion of the general will, because of its meta-rationality, admits of a romantic, intuitive, even dictatorial or tyrannical interpretation. But Rousseau's view does not lead *necessarily* to totalitarianism. It is merely an argument that other forms of government besides democracy are appropriate under certain conditions. Even so, there is no denying the disquieting fact that Hitler did claim to be the "voice" of the German people. If he had used Rousseauistic terms he could have said he represented the general will. Long before Hitler, Napoleon Bonaparte, one of the great dictators in European history, was an ardent believer in Rousseau and thought that he, rather than the revolutionaries, fulfilled the role Rousseau had assigned the lawgiver. He was the *legislateur* and the *dictateur* rolled into one. Therefrom sprang his personal interest in the great French *Code Civil*. From this evidence you can perceive the uncomfortable conclusion that a bridge leads from Rousseau into autocratic regimes, including totalitarian dictatorships. I am still convinced, however, that it is more wrong than right to link Rousseau with totalitarianism. The reason is Rousseau's emphasis on compassion, whereas one of the most distressing features of totalitarianism is its utter disregard of compassion. Totalitarians sneer at it as bourgeois sentimentality and humanitarianism. Millions are killed without compunction in the name of an abstract ideology.

Rousseau himself did not extend this compassion to the world-wide community of man. His introduction to a famous plan for the maintenance of peace, developed earlier in the century by the Abbé Saint Pierre, takes a rather skeptical view. In a study of this aspect of Rousseau, Stanley Hoffmann has said that "there is no lasting shelter between the state of war and the utopia of isolated communities." It was Kant who went beyond Rousseau in proclaiming it a necessary corollary of the categorical imperative that "there shall not be war." Although Rousseau had assumed that there was an ever-present possibility of violence, or a "state of war" (as had Hobbes), Kant believes that a state of permanent peace is not only conceivable, but may gradually be realized through an effective political organization of mankind. If the categorical imperative is a sound interpretation of man's moral nature, then he will be impelled toward extending political order to include all men and thereby eliminate the need for the use of political violence. I cannot here trace for you the argument of Kant's immortal essay— and its theme is one to which Kant gave some attention in all his major works—but one point is crucial, namely its insistence upon the equality of all men in the search for peace. The key principle of universal hospitality is the absolute antithesis to war and imperial domination. Hospitality for Kant means "the right of a foreigner not to be treated with hostility. . . ." But from this basic position, Kant arrives at the conception which underlies the United Nations and all other efforts at international organization. He wrote "The narrower or wider community of all nations on earth has in fact progressed so far that a violation of law and right in one place is felt in all others." In short, the national community is not the ultimate community. Men everywhere on earth have ultimately the same rights, that is to say, the claim to basic equality. We are yet very far from having reached that stage. But who would deny that we have gone forward since Kant wrote in 1796? He himself speaks at the conclusion of the *Essay* of only "an infinitely gradual approximation." Yet he insists that the eternal peace "is no empty idea, but a task which gradually solved, steadily approaches its end." Behind the clash of interests and ideologies a kind of continuing dialogue between Rousseau and Kant has been perceived. Let us hope that Kant's position eventually prevails. It is the conclusion to the basic problems of politics studied in this course.

READINGS, SUGGESTED AND REQUIRED

Lectures 11 and 12:

REQUIRED READING:

J. S. MILL, "Considerations on Representative Government," Ch. 3, in *The Philosophy of J. S. Mill* (Modern Library).

JOHN PLAMENATZ, *Man and Society,* Vol. I, Ch. 10 (McGraw-Hill).

J. J. ROUSSEAU, *The Social Contract* and the *Discourses* (Everyman). (You may omit the first "Discourse.")

SUGGESTIONS FOR FURTHER READING:

JOHN W. CHAPMAN, *Rousseau—Totalitarian or Liberal?* (Columbia University Press).

ALFRED COBBAN, *Rousseau and the Modern State* (Shoe String).

ROBERT DAHL, *Preface to Democratic Theory* (Phoenix).

C. J. FRIEDRICH, *Inevitable Peace* (Harvard).

C. J. FRIEDRICH, *The New Image of the Common Man* (Little, Brown).

CHARLES W. HENDEL, *Jean-Jacques Rousseau: Moralist* (Library of Liberal Arts, Bobbs-Merrill).

LEONARD KRIEGER, *The German Idea of Freedom: History of a Political Tradition* (Beacon Press).

SANFORD LAKOFF, *Equality in Political Philosophy* (Harvard).

ALEXANDER D. LINDSAY, *Kant* (E. Benn Ltd.).

J. J. ROUSSEAU, *Emile.*

GIOVANNI SARTORI, *Democratic Theory* (Praeger).

J. SCHUMPETER, *Capitalism, Socialism and Democracy,* Chs. 21–23 (Harper & Row).

RICHARD H. TAWNEY, *Equality* (Barnes & Noble).

A. DE TOCQUEVILLE, *Democracy in America,* Cf. Mill, "M. de Tocqueville on Democracy in America," in *The Philosophy of J. S. Mill* (Modern Library).

During the "Reading Period" two books are suggested:

I. KANT, *On Eternal Peace,* in *The Philosophy of Kant,* ed. Friedrich (Modern Library).

FREDERICK WATKINS, *The Political Tradition of the West* (Harvard).

Index